THE LANGUAGE OF PERJURY CASES

THE LANGUAGE OF PERJURY CASES

Roger W. Shuy

OXFORD
UNIVERSITY PRESS

OXFORD
UNIVERSITY PRESS

Oxford University Press, Inc., publishes works that further
Oxford University's objective of excellence
in research, scholarship, and education.

Oxford New York
Auckland Cape Town Dar es Salaam Hong Kong Karachi
Kuala Lumpur Madrid Melbourne Mexico City Nairobi
New Delhi Shanghai Taipei Toronto

With offices in
Argentina Austria Brazil Chile Czech Republic France Greece
Guatemala Hungary Italy Japan Poland Portugal Singapore
South Korea Switzerland Thailand Turkey Ukraine Vietnam

Published by Oxford University Press, Inc.
198 Madison Avenue, New York, NY 10016

www.oup.com

Library of Congress Cataloging-in-Publication Data
Shuy, Roger W.
The language of perjury cases / Roger W. Shuy.
p. cm.
Includes bibliographical references and index.
ISBN 978-0-19-979538-3 (alk. paper)
1. Perjury—United States.
2. Forensic linguistics—United States.
I. Title.
KK9420.S55 2011
325.73'0234—dc22 2010054107

I wish to give special thanks to my daughter, Katie Shuy, for her editing and proofreading assistance in the writing of this book. Her skills and suggestions were extremely helpful. I also want to thank Professor Larry Solan of the Brooklyn Law School and Professors Jeff Rentz and Fritz Snyder of the University of Montana Law School for helping me try to understand some of the legal aspects of perjury. I can only hope that I was an apt learner.

CONTENTS

SECTION III
PERJURY AND THE ILL-FATED SHIPPING VESSEL, *KHIAN SEA*

SECTION IV
PERJURY CHARGES ACROSS LANGUAGES AND CULTURES

SECTION V
PERJURY CASES WITH ADEQUATE INTELLIGENCE ANALYSIS

THE LANGUAGE OF PERJURY CASES

Introduction

Back in the days when I taught classes I often challenged my students to tell me any area of human life that was *not* relevant to linguistics. I never got a single valid answer, but I don't mean to say that linguists have fully explored all of the potential possible connections and applications. They have made many contributions to education and medical communication, and there are signs that some progress is being made in other fields, such as politics and business. During the past few decades, linguists also have been exploring the relationship of linguistics to many issues relating to law, including undercover criminal sting operations such as bribery, money laundering, solicitation to murder, identification of authors and speakers, threat messages, and narcotics possession and sales. They've also written about police interrogations, confessions given by suspects, trademark infringement, contract disputes, bureaucratic language that invites lawsuits, deceptive trade practices, product liability, copyright battles, various types of discrimination, and defamation. Many linguists have also analyzed legal language, statutes, and the way language is used in the courtroom. By now it has become clear that linguistic tools and analysis are highly relevant to all areas of law. This should not be surprising, because law is mostly about language.

In this book, I turn my attention to the way linguists can use their analytical tools in legal procedures relating to charges of perjury. I've served either as an expert witness or consultant to lawyers in hundreds of cases during the past three decades, and I've preserved files from almost all of them. I store them by case type and when I'm ready to write about them, I retrieve the banker's boxes marked by that case type, review the relevant cases, and select a few to illustrate the usefulness of linguistic analysis as a book. This book reprises some of the perjury cases I've worked on during my career.

I've found no good way to discuss the linguistic aspects of a case without first providing readers with relevant background information. Sometimes the case background is so complicated that it takes a few thousand words to describe it adequately. But language analysis depends on social and linguistic context and so this is the way I begin each chapter. Readers may find these stories interesting in themselves, but the major reason I tell them is to provide context for the analysis that follows.

I've divided this book on linguistics and perjury into five sections. Section I sets the stage. Chapter 1 briefly describes perjury law and the requirements for the prosecutor and triers of the facts in such cases. Chapter 2 outlines the linguistic tools that I have found useful when I work on perjury cases. Perjury indictments and prosecutions are based on two important features of science: effective intelligence gathering and effective intelligence analysis. These threads are present throughout the book. Linguistics, like all sciences, has these same requirements, so connecting linguistics to the way evidence is gathered and analyzed is only natural.

Section II (chapters 3 through 6) outlines the way linguistic analysis was applied to four very different perjury cases in which the prosecutors had first performed rather inadequate intelligence analysis before going to trial with their cases.

Section III describes two cases (chapters 7 and 8) that continue the focus on ineffective prosecutorial intelligence analysis. I placed them in a separate section here because of their complex and unfamiliar contextual background information. In addition, it is unusual that two separate trials were held at different times with different lawyers on what was essentially the same legal issue.

Section IV (chapters 9 and 10) deals with cross-cultural perjury cases in which the defendants had some knowledge of English, but were unable to make themselves clear enough to avoid indictments of perjury. Although the legal system is making some progress in dealing with bilingual interpreters for non-English speakers, there has been little focus on the language problems caused by fairly competent non-native speakers of English who transfer aspects of their native language and culture to the English used in the legal process, including perjury cases.

Most of the cases described in this book give evidence of serious problems in either gathering the intelligence or in analyzing it. But in the hope that such cases are exceptions to the rule, Section V (chapters 11 through 13) includes three perjury cases in which one or both of these requirements were fully met. Since I make no claim that prosecutions for perjury are always wrong, I hope that by including these chapters in which a prosecutor, a judge, and a district attorney halted prospective prosecutions that were based on faulty intelligence gathering and analysis, I will provide a balance to the eight case descriptions that point out the ways that analysis of language showed that these prosecutions were badly analyzed and managed.

I recognize that readers may be disappointed to not learn the outcomes of some of these cases. As I have said repeatedly in other books and articles, winning or losing is not the concern of expert witnesses and consultants, who should always remain outside the advocacy system. For this reason, I do not often include case outcomes.

I should also explain why the cases described here take only the perspective of the defense. One reason for this is that prosecutors seldom call on linguistic expert witnesses or even ask them to consult on their criminal cases. I have consulted with the prosecution in only a small percentage of the over five hundred cases I've worked on during the past thirty years, and I have been called to testify for the prosecution in only one of them. In other cases, such as the one described in chapter 13, I was hired by the prosecutor to review the government's evidence and to help him decide whether or not to pursue the indictment to trial. I have also reviewed the language evidence in scores of criminal cases and had to tell the defense lawyers that this evidence was so overwhelmingly bad for their clients that my best advice was to take whatever plea they could get. In these cases, linguistic analysis and testimony would have done them absolutely no good.

Finally, it should be made clear that I was paid for my services in all but the case described in chapter 9, which is a report of another linguist's work.

SECTION I
Perjury and linguistics

To understand how language relates to perjury, it's first necessary to know the essential elements of perjury law. This book is not a treatise on law, but I've tried to give some necessary basic outlines of U.S. perjury law in chapter 1, including the requirements of prosecutors and judges when perjury cases are brought and tried. This chapter also introduces the important roles played by good intelligence gathering and intelligence analysis when people are charged with perjury.

Chapter 2 describes the role of linguistics in perjury cases. Although it is common for prosecutors and defense lawyers to pay close attention to individual words, phrases, and sentences, one thesis of this book is that they could benefit from beginning their analyses of perjury evidence by examining the larger language units, because the smaller language units can be better understood when they are seen in the contexts where they occur. This suggests that they should identify the participants' expectations about the speech event itself, as well as the schemas and agendas as revealed through the topics of the participants, the language choices the speakers make when they respond to other speakers, and their conversational strategies. Once these larger language units are identified and analyzed, the intelligence analysts then can better benefit from examining the smaller units of language, because these are embedded in the larger units from which their meaning can be clarified. By smaller units, I mean the intended meanings of words and phrases, the vagueness and ambiguity that occurs, the speaker's or writer's referencing processes, and the way that the recency principle may or may not create misunderstanding between the participants in those conversations.

The relationship between linguistics and perjury has not received much attention from linguists, but a good place to begin is with *Speaking of Crime* (2005), by Lawrence Solan and Peter Tiersma, both of whom are professional linguists as well as professors of law. Chapter 11 of their book should be required reading for linguists and lawyers alike, particularly because of its lucid analyses of the U.S. Supreme Court's treatment of alleged perjury in the case of *Bronston v. United States* and the impeachment trial of President William Clinton. Tiersma's article, "The language of perjury: 'Literal truth,' ambiguity, and the false statement requirement" (1990) is another very important resource on this topic.

(1)
Perjury and proof of perjury

In every civil case in which I have served as a consultant or expert witness, I first had to deal with the inevitable deposition. Depositions are more taxing on witnesses than courtroom testimony, largely because in most cases there is no judge or jury present, sometimes making the lawyers' normal patterns of decorum and politeness fall by the wayside. One of the scariest moments for me came at the very beginnings of most of my depositions, when the opposing lawyer would ask me if I understood that if my answers were not truthful, I would be subject to perjury charges. Even though I realized that they were simply trying to distract me or throw me off from the start, this always gave me a lump in my throat. Advising (or perhaps threatening) me in this way was frightening even though I knew it was very unlikely that anything I had to say in a deposition could meet the materiality level required for a real perjury charge. I could get a date wrong, forget something, or mix up some names or places that could indicate some level of my confusion, my memory lapse, or even my incompetence, but this wasn't likely to rise to the level of perjury under any definition. So what then does perjury really mean?

Historically, perjury has been considered an odious crime. There is considerable justification for this judgment because perjury threatens the fair and effective administration of justice (Gershman 1981, 636). Without strong laws against perjury, crimes of bribery, extortion, and obstruction of justice could otherwise be shielded.

At common law, perjury was "the willful giving, under oath, in a judicial proceeding or course of justice, of false testimony material to the issue or the point of inquiry" (J. Bishop, 2 *Commentaries on the Criminal Law* § 860, 1858). The "course of justice" referred to a proceeding, such as a creditor's examination of a judgment debtor or a grand jury inquiry that was related to judicial proceedings. The general understanding of perjury is reflected in state and federal statutes and in various courts' explanations of them. For example, the federal statutory definition in 18 United States Code Section § 1621 declares:

> § 1621. Perjury generally
> Whoever—
> (1). having taken an oath before a competent tribunal, officer, or person, in any case in which a law of the United States authorizes an oath to be administered, that he will testify, declare, depose, or certify truly, or that any written testimony, declaration, deposition, or certificate by him subscribed, is true, willfully and contrary to such oath states or subscribes any material matter which he does not believe to be true; or
> (2). in any declaration, certificate, verification, or statement under penalty of perjury as permitted under section 1746 of title 28, United States Code, willfully subscribes as true any material matter which he does not believe to be true:
> is guilty of perjury and shall, except as otherwise expressly provided by law, be fined under this title or imprisoned not more than five years, or both. This section is applicable whether the statement or subscription is made within or without the United States.

Under §1621(1), six elements are required to prove that persons have committed perjury:

1. The speaker makes an oral statement.
2. That statement is false.

3. The speaker makes that statement under oath.
4. The speaker knows that the statement is false.
5. The speaker makes that statement before a judicial proceeding.
6. The speaker's statement relates to a material matter.

Perjury is not just any misstatement made while under oath. The Supreme Court of the United States has explained:

> A witness testifying under oath or affirmation violates this section if she gives false testimony concerning a material matter with the willful intent to provide false testimony, rather than the result of confusion, mistake, or faulty memory (*United States v. Dunnigan,* 507 U.S. 87, 94 (1993)).

Even more simply put, perjury means, "swearing to what the witness knows to be untrue." It's lying under oath, commonly in the context of giving testimony in court. Such lying is different from simply making a mistake, because the law requires that any perjurious statement be intentional. It is different from evasion or half-truth because the perjury must be about some matter that the witness believes to be false; creating a misleading impression through indirection, while dishonest, is not perjury. The false statement also must be material, meaning that the falsehood has the potential to influence the outcome of trials or other official proceedings.

There is a further difference between perjury and false statements, because perjury connotes corruption and recalcitrance, while false swearing, usually made in a written statement while not under oath, connotes mere falsehood without moral judgment (Garner 1995). This difference is recognized in some jurisdictions but not in others. In the federal jurisdiction, a false statement not under oath can be as damning as perjury (18 U.S.C. § 1001). In fact, if you falsely deny committing a crime during an interview with a federal officer (what is called an "exculpatory no," a mere "I didn't do it"), you can be imprisoned for five years and be fined $10,000 (*Brogan v. United States,* 552 U.S. 398 (1998)). For example, this was the crime that eventually convicted Martha Stewart.

Prosecution for making false statements is not limited to perjury cases. For example, a person who falsely injures someone's reputation can be prosecuted for defamation. Statements that invade the privacy of others by adding false statements to the life story of that person can also lead to charges of making false statements. Trade libel, which reduces the reputation of that company by making knowingly untrue statements about it, can also result in charges of making false statements.

Linguistic analysis fits into this picture because the determination of perjury rests on the language used by both the questioner and the person who answers, which in turn has to be judged by the jury or, in bench trials, by the judge. The problem is how to determine whether perjury actually took place or whether a speaker simply made a mistake.

In grand jury testimony, the witness has several requirements that run counter to the conventional and predictable speech events in life. For example, witnesses are not permitted to challenge questions that they believe to be incompetent or irrelevant or questions that seem to exceed the questioner's authority. The only role of witnesses is to testify about what they know (*Blair v. United States,* 250 U.S. 282 (1919)). Nor are witnesses permitted to remain silent before a grand jury unless they are subject to valid Fifth Amendment claims, and the prosecutor is not obligated to advise witnesses of the dangers of testifying falsely (*United States v. Mandujano,* 425 U.S. 564, 581–82 (1976)).

The possibilities of errors about whether or not perjury has taken place appear in several places that are not relevant to the application of linguistic analysis. First, there is the requirement that the witness be under oath. It may sound surprising, but there have been occasions in which a witness testified without first being sworn. Sometimes the person giving the oath is not qualified to do so. This arises more frequently in out-of-court proceedings, as in depositions and in those "courses of justice" referred to in the common law definitions of perjury. These can be of little interest to linguists.

On the other hand, the language of some witnesses, particularly those with limited intelligence or those whose command of the language is poor, might not express a clear understanding of the oath, providing an opportunity for linguistic analysis. Another potentially linguistic issue arises when the question asked is of poor quality.

While the crime of perjury requires that the falsehood be material, proof of perjury need not show that the witnesses knew that their answers would be material. Witnesses must only know that their answers are false. This gives rise to several possibilities. The question may be sufficiently unclear with respect to a material matter. In other words, when witnesses give knowingly false answers to questions that can be understood to call for information that is not material, it raises an issue of fact as to the materiality of those answers, which relates to law, logic, and the language used.

A more common opportunity for linguistic analysis relates to questions that are insufficiently clear to witnesses. That is, witnesses may believe they are giving true answers to questions as they understood them. This is not in itself perjury. But because we don't have a clear window into the minds of witnesses, it's difficult for the courts or linguists to tell whether people intended to give false answers to the questions as understood by the questioner or to give truthful answers to the questions as understood by the witnesses.

This problem doesn't happen very often, because there is normally another attorney or a judge present to ensure that the questions are clear. In a trial, all concerned are supposed to be interested in reaching an accurate outcome. It is not unusual, therefore, for the non-questioning attorney to object that the other lawyer's questions are unclear or for a judge to interject for the same reason. In a deposition, which is not attended by a judge, the attorney who is not asking the questions can place objections to questions on the deposition record. Smart, alert witnesses will request clarification of unclear questions at the time they are asked. Smart questioners will then clarify. When neither takes place, witnesses can be insulated from perjury charges by their own attorney's references to the written transcript of their testimony, asserting that certain of the other attorney's questions were unclear.

The situation is a bit different in grand jury proceedings, however. In usual grand jury hearings, only the prosecutor, the witness, and the grand jury (which does not act as a referee) are present. As a general rule, even if witnesses are targets of the grand jury investigation, they have no right to have counsel present. This means that a grand jury inquiry is fraught with peril for such witnesses. It also means that the questions must be clear enough that the witnesses and the grand juries are on the same page with the prosecutors.

The following summarizes the aspects of perjury that are of potential interest for linguistic analysis. For the most part, perjury charges arise from earlier testimony at a criminal trial, or before a grand jury in a criminal case. I therefore refer to the questioner as "the prosecutor." However, perjury can also arise as a result of false testimony in civil cases, whether at a trial, at a hearing, or in a deposition.

WHEN A PROSECUTOR SHOULD BRING A PERJURY CASE

- To sustain a perjury charge, prosecutors have to demonstrate careful and clear questioning and be able to demonstrate that the defendants *were aware of the meaning* of the questions and the falsity of their answers. For grand jury testimony to support a perjury charge, *the meaning of the prosecutor's question must be clear,* and a court should not assume a particular meaning.

- The indictment must evidence a *meeting of the minds* of the prosecutors, defendants, and grand jury in order to properly charge defendants with perjury based on their grand jury statements.
- If a prosecutor's question is *excessively vague* or *fundamentally ambiguous,* the answer to the question should not form the basis of a perjury or false statement prosecution. Although a prosecutor should be careful to establish a clear meaning as to the critical charge, *some words are so common* that there cannot be any ambiguity.
- While a prosecutor should use precise questions for responses to those questions to support a perjury charge, it is sufficient that requisite precision *can be inferred* from the context.
- An indictment charging the defendant with perjury should set forth the particular falsehood *with clarity,* along with the government's factual basis for the charge.

WHAT SHOULD BE LEFT FOR THE JURY OR JUDGE

- A jury in a perjury prosecution *should not have to speculate* (1) about the prosecutor's meaning, (2) about the defendant's meaning, and (3) about the grand jury questioning that gives rise to a charge.
- Where words or phrases of common usage form the predicate of a perjury charge and are arguably *susceptible to more than one construction,* it is the job of the triers of the facts to determine whether the witnesses and their examiners held a *shared understanding.*
- Common sense meanings of the words used should be considered, in light of the knowledge of the witness at the time of

the testimony, in determining whether a challenged statement is *sufficiently specific* to support perjury charges.

- In determining whether statements are sufficiently clear to support a perjury conviction, it is necessary to consider the defendants' own uses of the challenged terms in order to determine whether they *understood the meaning* of the questions posed.
- Perjury cannot be sustained by *lifting a statement of the accused out of its immediate context* and thus giving it a meaning wholly different from what its context clearly shows.
- The issue of whether a question is fatally ambiguous, and thus may not constitute perjury, should be determined from *the context* of the interaction.

In summary, the prosecutor needs to ask questions in a clear and unambiguous way and have the factual basis for comparison with known facts in order to determine that the witness's answers are untrue in a context in which witnesses can understand what is being asked of them. The jury or judge should not speculate about what is meant by both prosecutors and witnesses, and they also have to determine whether the language used by prosecutors was specific enough to witnesses that a perjury charge can be supported. Furthermore, the jury and judge have to view the language evidence in the overall *context* of the questions and answers.

If there is anything in law that invites linguistic analysis, it is perjury. So how is perjury proved?

INTELLIGENCE GATHERING AND ANALYSIS

When prosecutors decide whether or not to charge perjury, they typically carry out an intelligence analysis of the evidence, which in perjury cases compares the known (or suspected) factual evidence with the language used by the defendant. I have suggested elsewhere that intelligence analysis is central to investigations in law cases (Shuy 1990, 125–26). To be effective, such analysis has to precede any accusation or indictment of perjury. When the charge of perjury is based on testimony under oath, the obvious way to proceed is to analyze the language used by witnesses and to compare it with the other evidence in the case. If needed, linguists are available to help with such intelligence analysis.

Intelligence analysis is often thought to be the sole territory of organizations such as the CIA in the United States or the SIS, M16 in the United Kingdom, although it is also sometimes used by commercial businesses as they deal with competitors. It seems obvious, however, that intelligence analysis also is central to the legal context, where it has the same purpose of discovering ambiguity, false leads, incomplete information of messages, and the production of reasonable, accurate interpretations from potentially confusing data. Andrews and Peterson (1990) provide a detailed description of the relevance of intelligence analysis for police interrogations and for eliciting confessions, much of which can be traced to the seminal work of Godfrey and Harris (1971). I suggest here that good intelligence analysis also directly leads to more accurate analyses of legal cases, including perjury.

One definition of intelligence analysis is: "that activity whereby meaning, actual or suggested...is derived through organizing and systematically examining diverse information" (Harris 1976, 30). An important primary step in good intelligence analysis is for the analyst to develop more than one hypothesis: "The analyst must formulate alternative hypotheses...to probe allegations and suggestions of criminal activity rather than to build an evidentiary case" (Harris 1976, 34). This suggests that analysts must be able to go against their own presuppositions, recognize the unlikely, and provide connections that are not immediately obvious to others.

In perjury cases, this means that prosecutors, as intelligence analysts, should not only have hypotheses of defendants' guilt, but also should explore hypotheses of innocence. According to a former intelligence analyst at the CIA's Directorate of Operations, the best use of information is to challenge the assumption that the analyst likes best (Heuer 1999). Failure to do this can lead to vast wastes of public resources, as I have noted elsewhere in such cases as the *United States v. John DeLorean*, the automobile manufacturer who was acquitted because the prosecutor's single hypothesis of guilt prevented him from exploring any alternative hypotheses (Shuy 1993, 73). This is similar to a syndrome of some law enforcement agencies that has been called "detective myopia." When interviewed about the FBI's anthrax investigation of Dr. Stephen J. Hatfill, former Los Angeles Police Chief Daryl F. Gates said that he believed that the agents became so focused on Hatfill that they lost their objectivity (Freed 2010, 52). Dr. Hatfill was never indicted, however, because the case against him was so thin.

Some of the attributes of good intelligence analysis include the ability to be impersonal and neutral, to be receptive to new data, to view the data in its context, to analyze inductively, and to be free from bias. In short, intelligence analysis follows the familiar and standard scientific principles of systematically collecting relevant and representative data, evaluating what is collected, analyzing all of it with the proper tools, and arriving at an informed conclusion that is accurate and generalizable. This is illustrated in a scientist's proposed research in the form of a research grant, where the proposal is soundly reviewed before the research even begins. If something is lacking in the proposal, the project is stopped at that point. If the proposal is supported by peer evaluations, the project may be funded and the research begins. After the research is completed, the scientists' conclusions are then carefully scrutinized and evaluated by other experts in that field.

In a similar way, criminal law cases also begin with an unresolved problem or issue that provides these same opportunities to gather evidence data that is systematically and accurately representative, a step called intelligence gathering, usually done by police departments or other law enforcement agencies. The next step, intelligence analysis, is carried out by the prosecutor who employs the most useful and appropriate analytical tools in order to reach accurate and proper conclusions. Different from the scientific process, however, is that the ultimate review and evaluation of this intelligence gathering and analysis is carried out by triers of the facts—juries or judges.

When scientists, law enforcement personnel or lawyers fail in their intelligence gathering and intelligence analysis efforts, it is often likely that they first hadn't gathered accurate or representative data systematically, that they failed to use the proper analytical tools and procedures, or, based on their data gathering and analysis, that they failed to reach an accurate and proper conclusion.

In science, the penalty for bad intelligence gathering and analysis leads to professional criticism by the scientist's peers, which in turn leads to embarrassment and possible loss of professional reputation. In contrast, the penalty for bad intelligence gathering and analysis of indicted defendants can (and should) lead to an acquittal when the jury or judge recognizes that the intelligence gathering and analyses are faulty or insufficient. Absent such judgment, defendants can be convicted when triers of the fact fail to recognize the shortcomings of that intelligence gathering and analysis process. From that point on, things become difficult, because when these triers of the facts make bad decisions, appealing the verdict is complex and time consuming. In contrast, good intelligence gathering and intelligence analysis can lead to the proper conviction of defendants if the evidence and analyses are accurate, convincing, and proper. By the same token, bad intelligence gathering and intelligence analysis can lead at best to wasted resources and at worst to false convictions.

The following chapters describe eleven actual perjury cases, in nine of which I was retained by the defense lawyer to analyze the language used by both the prosecutors and the defendants to determine whether perjury was actually indicated. In one case, I was retained by the district attorney for the same purpose. Another chapter describes an analysis made by different linguist in a perjury case. Intelligence analysis by the prosecution proved somewhat faulty in nine of these cases but was correct in two of them. I make no claim, however, that this ratio represents the common practice of prosecutions. Lawyers call on linguists for assistance only in cases in which there is sufficient reason to suspect something amiss in the charges. My only claim here is that in many such cases, lawyers and prosecutors could use the help of linguists.

(2) How linguists examine the language of perjury

One thing about perjury is certain: the duties of the prosecutor, jury, and judge, noted earlier, are basically about language use, meaning, and context:

- the defendant has to be aware of the prosecutor's meaning;
- the questions and answers have to be clear and unambiguous;
- there has to be a meeting of the minds about the meaning;
- commonly used words are not vague or ambiguous;
- the overall context of the questions and answers have to be considered;
- the prosecutor and jury can't speculate about the witness's meaning.

Linguists deal with issues of ambiguity and specificity of meaning, with language evidence about whether a person understands what is asked, with the difference between representations of fact versus opinions, with language characteristics in the role of speculation, with the significance of sociolinguistic and discourse context in interpreting meaning, with evidence of error-making versus intentionally deceptive language, and with the role of cultural and language differences in the interpretation of language use. This book illustrates some of the ways linguistic analysis contributes to the understanding and resolution of perjury cases, using the following brief descriptions of ten analytical tools, which are organized from broad to narrow language units, reflecting the analytical sequence that is preferable to follow: the speech event, the schemas of the participants, the speaker's agendas as revealed by their topics, their agendas as revealed by responses, the role of the cooperative principle, the speech acts used, the speakers' conversational strategies, the recency principle, language ambiguity, and word semantics.

THE SPEECH EVENT AND CONTEXT

Gumperz (1990, 9) defines speech events as recurring occasions in which there are "tacitly understood rules of preference, unspoken conventions as to what counts as valid and what information may or may not be introduced." He gives some examples of speech events, including interviews (job, counseling, psychiatric, governmental), committee negotiations, courtroom interrogations, formal hearings, and public debates and discussions. He points out that "the participant structure of such events thus reflects the real power asymmetry underneath the surface equality, a serious problem when the lesser communicator does not know the rules." In addition to his list of speech events, I have added the speech events of the business negotiation interview, for which the bribery speech event is a close relative (Shuy 1993, 21–23) and the sales event (Shuy 1998b, 146–49).

The courtroom exchange in which the speaker is under oath, as Gumperz notes, constitutes one identifiable type of speech event. It certainly contains a power asymmetry, and it becomes complicated when the participant who has lesser status does not know the speech event rules. There is hardly any reason to expect courtroom exchanges between a prosecutor and a defendant to be cordial and pleasant. The prosecutor's sworn duty is to get to the truth of a matter, even when doing this suggests a harsh attack, while defendants often find themselves taking a continuously defensive stance.

Trials and hearings provide the usual venues for this type of speech event. They are conventionally governed by a rigid system that allows only the lawyer to choose the topics to be answered, ask the questions, and control the entire interaction. In contrast, witnesses cannot introduce topics or ask any questions other than to request clarification when prosecutors are unclear. In this speech event, all of the power and control is on the prosecutors' side of the witness box. The perjury cases discussed in chapters involving a businessman (chapter 3), two shipping executives (chapters 7 and 8), a union representative (chapter 10), and a priest (chapter 13) illustrate the influence of this speech event context on the participants' interactions.

Perjury law also indicates that the issue of whether a question is fatally ambiguous and thus may not support a perjury charge should be ascertained from the context of the interrogation. The first task here is to determine the overall interactive context, including the speech event itself, in relation to the immediate, contiguous context of the lawyer's individual questions and the defendant's individual answers, because understood meanings often are built gradually over time throughout the entire speech event. If the participants assign different meanings to a given word, expression, or sentence throughout the exchange under oath, the contextual meaning is that of the entire colloquy, not just an isolated individual question-and-answer pair.

SCHEMAS

When people converse with each other, they have expectations about what is being said that are based on the way they already know and understand how the world works. They have prerecorded scripts in their heads and when something is said that reminds them of these scripts, the script can take over and color their perception of what the other person is saying. Schemas are defined as "mental representations of some aspect of experience, based on prior experience and memory, structured in such a way as to facilitate (and sometimes distort) perception, cognition, and the ability to draw inferences or to interpret new information in terms of existing knowledge" (Coleman and Kay 1981, 26–44). Speakers often say just enough to trigger a schema in the minds of listeners, who then use that schema as they try to make sense out of what they hear from that point onward. Unfortunately, what the listeners puzzle out is sometimes not what the speakers intended, resulting in conflicting schemas, something like trains passing in the night. Several cases in this book, especially chapters 7 and 8 (the two shipping executives), illustrate the workings of schemas in the minds of the prosecutor and the defendant.

AGENDAS REVEALED BY TOPICS

One of the most useful tools of discourse analysis is that of the topics and agendas of the speakers (Shuy 1982, 1990, 1993, 1998a, 2001, 2005). The best clues available for determining speakers' intentions are derived from the topics (conversational subjects) they bring up and recycle in language interactions. When these topics are accumulated and classified into themes, they provide clues to what is foremost in the speakers' minds, their agendas. The topics they do *not* introduce are almost equally useful to notice, especially when those topics are the ones that they are accused of wanting to advance. The perjury cases of a lawyer (chapter 11), a failed businessman (chapter 3), a bungled bank loan (chapter 5) and a U.S. Senator (chapter 12) illustrate how topic and agenda analysis can provide useful clues to help understand the intentions of the speakers.

AGENDAS REVEALED BY RESPONSES TO TOPICS OF OTHERS

There are many ways for participants in verbal exchanges to respond to the topics of others. For example, they can express various degrees of agreement or disagreement, ranging from partial to total. They can answer questions completely or partially. They can say nothing at all or they can change the subject without responding to it (Shuy 1993, 66–68). These response strategies, whether used consciously or not, can provide useful clues to the intentions of the speakers.

THE COOPERATIVE PRINCIPLE

Successful human interaction is based on the cooperation of its participants. Despite any asymmetry of power and control, speakers in an exchange are expected to be cooperative. H. P. Grice (1975) outlined the principles upon which a cooperative exchange takes place, and linguists have been applying Grice's cooperative principle ever since his seminal work became available. In simplified terms, the four maxims of the cooperative principle are:

- be informative; say that which is required but don't say more than is required;
- be relevant and don't wander off topic;
- say what is true—be sincere; and
- be clear and orderly—don't be ambiguous or obscure.

These four maxims provide a touchstone for examining the language used by both prosecutors and defendants in perjury cases. At times, these maxims tend to overlap each other. For example, in response to prosecutors' questions, witnesses can be cooperative by saying something that is true, but at the same time they can be uncooperative when this truthful information is not germane to the question asked, causing the response to violate the maxim of relevance. Similarly, a truthful answer can be so obscure or ambiguous that it simultaneously violates the maxims of informativeness and relevance. Finally, the answer can be simply untrue, and when proven to be untrue, this also violates the maxims of informativeness and relevance.

These maxims of communication apply not only to the subordinate person who is required to follow the communicative rules of the courtroom, but also to prosecutors, who are equally bound by them. Since prosecutors are in control of the speech event, they get to ask the questions. Although they are not obliged to provide information, their questions have to be sincere, relevant to the topic, and, perhaps most important of all in perjury cases, clear and unambiguous.

Witnesses normally are charged with perjury when they offer an untrue statement under oath, violating the cooperative principle's requirement to contribute only that which is true and sincere. The other maxims, informativeness, relevance, and clarity, are not in themselves a necessary basis for a perjury charge, but such violations of the cooperative principle can become avenues that set the table for later accusations of perjury. Witnesses who answer a question saying less than is required can be considered uncooperative, but at that point they usually have not yet perjured themselves. Witnesses whose answers are irrelevant, ambiguous, unclear, or fail to be orderly also violate the cooperative principle, but they too have not yet committed perjury. The same can be said about witnesses who are informative about only part of the question asked them. This can (and does) happen because the speech event is a legal procedure in which the context is adversarial and where it can expected that both parties will parry and thrust, trying not to yield to each other. When witnesses give partial, irrelevant, or ambiguous answers, they invite prosecutors to ask follow-up questions that, depending on the answer, can lead to a charge of perjury, as in the cases of a failed businessman (chapter 3), and two shipping executives (chapters 7 and 8).

SPEECH ACTS

Beginning with the work of Austin (1962), later developed by Searle (1969), and up to the present day, speech acts, the functions performed by utterances, are often central to the study of continuous spoken and written discourse. Some utterances, called performatives, are equivalent to actions, as when a person says "I promise," "I apologize," or "I now pronounce you husband and wife." Speech acts are the effects of utterances produced by the speaker and perceived by the hearer. The language act that the speaker performs is called an illocutionary act, including such things as warning, advising, promising, thanking, and many others. The effect that the speaker's utterance has on the listener is called the perlocutionary effect. These speech acts have specific requirements for being successful or unsuccessful, as seen in the in the cases involving political contributions (chapter 4) and lawyer/client interviews (chapter 11).

CONVERSATIONAL STRATEGIES

In courtroom exchanges, it may appear that questions and answers operate separately and independently, but this is not always the case. The way a question is asked can influence, even determine, the answer that is given. Although in most everyday conversation this usually makes little difference, questioning strategies can have serious consequences in the courtroom. The courts have long recognized the problems caused by leading questions, ones that suggest the answer to the person being questioned. In Anglo-American law, such questions are permissible only in cross-examination (Garner 1995). Seldom discussed, however, is the problem that occurs when questioners ask multiple questions during the same turn of talk or when they ask a question without providing follow-up information that can clarify it. In tape-recorded undercover operations, this can lead to what I have identified as the "hit-and-run" strategy, a close linguistic relative of the recency principle (Shuy 2005, 21–22). Examples of the way prosecutors use this strategy are illustrated in chapters dealing with the union representative (chapter 10) and the state legislator (chapter 4).

RECENCY PRINCIPLE

When presented with an uninterrupted series of statements or questions, listeners tend to respond to the most recent (last one) in the series (Cuetos & Mitchell 1988; Gibson et al. 1996). This often happens in normal conversation, where the stakes are not high and loss of the missed topic can be easily repaired. But in exchanges that have legal consequences, the speaker can appear to be evasive or malingering. If the missed topic is crucial, a non-response can be interpreted very differently from the way it was intended.

AMBIGUITY

I am quick to observe that most judges and lawyers are highly competent in both using and analyzing language, but they are considerably less skilled at language analysis than linguists, as most of the cases described in this book demonstrate. For example, they often believe that some words are so common that they can't possibly produce any ambiguity, as when the judge denied the defense motion for a summary judgment in the case of the state legislator (chapter 4). The legislator gave clear evidence that he understood the meaning of the word "reimburse" in a way that seriously differed from that of the prosecutor. The judge did not agree:

> Words clear on their face can be interpreted in various ways when subjected to ingenious scrutiny after the fact. The words used were to be understood in their common sense, not as they might be warped by sophistry or twisted in pilpul.

After some effort, I managed to discover the definition of "pilpul," a penetrating investigation, disputation, and drawing of conclusions, especially in Talmudic studies. It seems ironic that this judge argued for the common sense, everyday meaning of words while at the same time using an expression that falls far short of having a common sense, everyday meaning.

The judge's objection to "scrutiny after the fact" in this opinion was also strange, since the only time that evidence can be analyzed is after it has come into existence—meaning after the fact. Even more interesting, however, is that the participants' disputed understanding of the word, "reimburse," occurred *during* the testimony, when the prosecutor and the witness assigned and applied different meanings of that word. The linguist's work was to scrutinize what the participants could mean and understand *during* that speech event, not after the fact.

It would appear that some judges view linguistic analysis as mere sophistry, a term that *Merriam-Webster's New Collegiate Dictionary* defines as "subtly deceptive reasoning or argumentation." I suppose we can be thankful that the *American Heritage Dictionary* prefaces the word "plausible" to "reasoning and argumentation" in its definition. It also seems unreasonable to linguists that without professional help from specialists in semantics and lexicography, judges like this one can make final decisions about whether meaning is so common that there can be no possible misunderstanding, while at the same time calling semantic analysis mere "sophistry." The road ahead for linguistic analysis to be accepted in some courts may be steeper than we imagined.

There are many ways that language provides for clarifying and repairing utterances that are not fully understood. As will be noted in the various cases reported in this book, the most obvious way is for either party to simply request clarification. The failures of prosecutors to request clarification about witnesses' vague or ambiguous answers are especially evident in the cases relating to political contributions (chapter 4), relating to a bank loan (chapter 5), and relating to the testimony of a shipping executive (chapter 7). Conversely (if not ironically), these witnesses requested clarification of the prosecutors' questions in their own attempts to resolve ambiguities. Other cases also describe the prosecutors' failures to try to resolve ambiguities that had arisen.

Ambiguities also result when a speaker's grammatical or semantic referencing is unclear. Semantic referencing occurs in language when a noun phrase in an utterance is associated with some other language entity. The most obvious problems come from pronoun references that don't clearly refer to their antecedents ("it," "you," and "they" are common problems). Other types of referencing confusion can stem from grammatical features such as English grammatical concord rule violations, as evidenced in the interview of a union representative (chapter 10) and a lawyer's interview with his clients (chapter 11).

The importance of the recency principle (listeners respond to the most recent parts of a sentence and ignore the earlier parts) in understanding referencing is shown in the recorded evidence of a businessman (chapter 5). Other problems with mutual understandability are seen in the perjury cases involving bankruptcy (chapter 3), political contributions (chapter 4), and a lawyer/client interview (chapter 11). Perhaps the most complex examples of failing to achieve mutual understandability occur with defendants whose first language is not English but who have still managed to learn to use it rather well. This can give listeners the mistaken impression that these non-native speakers are fully competent in the language, even though they are still influenced by their first language, as seen in a case reported by John Gumperz (chapter 9) and in the grand jury hearing of a union representative (chapter 10).

Misperceiving grammatical scope is another path that can lead to misunderstandings. Scope refers to that portion of a sentence that is affected by the linguistic operator present in that sentence. The operator is any grammatical element or adjunct that bears a scope relation to some part of its sentence, often involving such things as determiners, quantifiers, negation markers, tense, aspect, and mood. In a construction containing two scope-bearing elements, the one that comes first will generally have scope over the one that comes later (Huddleston & Pullum 2002, 794). Chapter 11 (a lawyer-client interview) illustrates how grammatical scope led to different interpretations about what was being discussed.

WORD SEMANTICS

Common conflicts also occur in perjury cases when prosecutors and defendants or witnesses hold different meanings of the same words. Cases that illustrate this problem include a bankruptcy application and hearing (chapter 3), problems relating to a political contribution (chapter 4), lack of clarity in the wording on a hunting license application (chapter 6), the testimony of two shipping agents (chapters 7 and 8), and the grand jury hearing of a union representative (chapter 10). Possible inferred meaning is illustrated in the recorded telephone call of a U.S. senator (chapter 12).

WHEN TO USE THESE TEN TOOLS

These ten tools are presented above in the same sequence that was followed in most of the linguistic analyses offered in the cases described in this book. Larger and broader language units are examined before smaller and narrower language units. The narrower language units, such as word meaning or ambiguity, are nested in the broader units of discourse and often their intended meanings can be derived from the overall context of the discourse.

My point here is that prosecutors, defense attorneys, and judges would do well to think about and carry out their intelligence analyses by beginning with the broader language discourse units, such as how the participants view the speech event, what their schemas are, how they reveal their agendas through the topics they introduce and recycle, what strategies they use in responding to the topics of others, how they handle the cooperative principle, and which felicitous speech acts they use. And, if they are really perceptive, lawyers can also notice how the recency principle is used and understood by the participants. I have found that it is more common for lawyers to place their focus on the narrower language units, such as ambiguity and word meanings, rather than the overall contextual meanings that are evident in the broader language units noted here. Narrow language units that at first blush look like "smoking guns" can often turn out to be considerably less than that.

DECEPTION AND INTENTIONALITY

In the midst of all this, intelligence analysts often need to assess whether speakers and writers are being deceptive or whether they are offering literal truth or figurative language. Linguistics can also help with this.

It's clear that some witnesses are deliberately deceptive. No science has the ability to reach inside a person's mind to discover with certainty whether or not they are lying (Shuy 1998; Galasinski 2000). Lying is a form of deception, a linguistic strategy for gaining compliance, an act of intentionally misleading in the same way that boasting, mockery, insinuation, propaganda, and certain commercial advertisements deliberately fail to reveal a full picture of the truth (Galasinki 2000). In short, deception is a form of linguistic manipulation, which can be accomplished intentionally by employing false presuppositions or implications, or passively by using silence or omission that allows the listener to develop a false understanding.

Truth or falsity is not always the issue, because a truthful and complete utterance can also be used deceptively, and a false and an incomplete utterance may be the product of the speaker's error or memory loss.

Lying involves producing an intentionally false statement that the speaker knows is false and that is intended to mislead the listener (Coleman & Kaye 1981), whereas deception is not always so straightforward. The speakers can't be lying, however, if they believe what they say is true, even though it is not. If this were the case, the astronomers who in 1928 affirmed that there were eight planets revolving around the earth would have to be considered liars (Fraser 1994).

Exaggerated language can be considered a form of lying, because it conveys more truth than is required. Presenting half-truths by minimizing the information can contain less truth than is required. Equivocation and evasion can contain indirectness, irrelevance, vagueness (uncertain meaning), or ambiguity (two or more possible meanings). These all violate Grice's maxims.

To address issues of lying and deception, linguists have tools that include conventional ways to analyze the sounds, grammar, and meaning of texts, as well as the more recent tools of discourse analysis, the maxims of cooperation, pragmatics, and speech acts. Some of these tools are illustrated in the bankruptcy case (chapter 3), but all perjury cases open the door to the possibility that defendants are being deceptive, based on their responses when they report memory loss, as in chapters 10 (a union representative) and 13 (a priest), in the professed lack of knowledge by the shipping executives (chapters 7 and 8), and in the language artifacts of confusing questions put to non-native English speakers (chapters 9 and 10). Sorting these types of answers into the proper categories of truth or deception is sometimes difficult to accomplish in perjury prosecutions.

LITERAL TRUTH

Solan and Tiersma (2005, 213) point out that one might expect the courts to take a relatively non-literal approach to determining the meaning of allegedly perjurious statements, but this is not the case. In the U.S. Supreme Court case of *Bronston v. United States* (409 U.S. 352, 353 1973), a bankruptcy hearing, the question was whether the witness could be convicted of perjury for testifying under oath about something that was literally true but not responsive to the question asked:

Q: Do you have any bank accounts in Swiss banks, Mr. Bronston?
A: No, sir.
Q: Have you ever?
A: The company had an account there for about six months, in Zurich.

Bronston's response to the first question was literally true, because even though he once held a personal account in a Swiss bank, he no longer did. He did not respond with personal information in his answer to the second question, choosing instead to report information about his company. This answer was literally true. So he really didn't provide any false information in either response.

He was convicted of perjury, however, because his answer falsely *implied* that he had never held such an account. After the appellate court upheld this verdict, Bronston's lawyers took it all the way to the U.S. Supreme Court, which unanimously reversed his conviction, concluding that the perjury statute refers to what a witness *states*, not to what a witness *implies*. The Court placed the onus on the prosecutor, whose job it was to notice that Bronston's answer violated the cooperative principle by offering a non-relevant response. Even if Bronston intended his answer to be evasive or deceptive, it was the prosecutor's job to probe the issue more deeply. Not surprisingly, for decades since this case, defense lawyers have tried to use the Bronston defense in their perjury cases. In fact, it was raised with little success in some of the cases described in this book, and it is particularly evident in the prosecutor's courtroom exchanges with the shipping executive (chapter 7) and elsewhere throughout this book.

SECTION II

Perjury charges with inadequate intelligence analysis

Intelligence collected in advance of indictments frames the eventual charges of perjury. Often this information is very convincing to the prosecutor and a trial soon follows. The types of data include written applications that contain alleged false statements, tapes and transcripts of official oral hearings, and undercover tape-recorded conversations.

Chapter 3 describes a bankruptcy case that contained not only information found in the applicant's alleged false statements, but also data from the oral hearing that followed. Together, these two sources of data comprised the prosecutor's intelligence gathering process. When the intelligence gathered from the first source, the application form, did not conform to the data gathered from the second source, the hearing, the intelligence analyst found himself in a quandary about which data source to use for charging the man with perjury. From discourse analysis, we know that when people are given the opportunity to repair or clarify their earlier statements, seeming errors can be resolved. But that didn't happen in this case, which strongly suggests that the prosecutor's intelligence analysis was at least questionable.

The language evidence in the case alleging the perjury of a politician, reported in chapter 4, consisted of tape-recordings and transcripts of his grand jury hearing, which turned out to be one of those trains-passing-in-the-night events where both the prosecutor and the defendant used the same word, but with very different understandings of its referential meaning. In *Bronston,* the U.S. Supreme Court had said it's the prosecutor's responsibility to seek clarification when ambiguity arises. That didn't happen in this case, producing questionable intelligence analysis.

Chapter 5 reports the problems of a real estate developer and manager who faced perjury charges for submitting false information on a bank loan for his company's financially failing shopping mall. Undercover tape-recordings of his conversations were made by his associates in the company, whose conversational strategies produced bad intelligence gathering that came under close scrutiny by the developer's defense team.

Chapter 6 describes the case of the confusing forms that are required for obtaining a hunting license and the subsequent perjury charges that were made when the applicant did not appear to understand what was asked. He was charged with submitting false statements. The lack of clarity on the license application forms was not recognized or acknowledged by the prosecutor, who proceeded to trial anyway, another example of faulty intelligence analysis.

This section shows not only that poor intelligence gathering and intelligence analysis preceded indictments, but also how linguistic analysis helped reveal this as a way of assisting lawyers for the defendants.

(3)
False statements in a bankruptcy case

The U.S. Bankruptcy Code § 521(2)(B) requires applicants to fill out Form 6B Schedules, called the Statement of Financial Affairs, and to submit this to the U.S. Bankruptcy Court. Within forty-five days after filing this statement, persons declaring bankruptcy are required to answer questions posed by the applicants' receivers and creditors in what is called a 341 hearing. A Dallas businessman, William Bolles, became financially devastated, so he filled out this 6B schedule and submitted it to the Bankruptcy Court on October 7, 1991. His hearing took place twenty-four days later.

Three and a half years after his hearing, in February 1995, the U.S. District Court for the Northern District of Texas indicted Bolles on five counts of bankruptcy fraud and perjury, based primarily on his Statement of Financial Affairs and on what Bolles said at his October 31, 1991, hearing, during which two of his creditors, his lawyer, his receiver, and the Court questioned him about his financial condition. An FBI agent was also recorded as being present, although the transcript does not report his contributions.

The five counts of Bolles's indictment were:

1. He reported that he had no financial accounts when in fact he had a brokerage account at Prudential Bache Securities.

2. He reported that he had no payments due to creditors when in fact he was making lease payments on a Jaguar automobile.
3. He did not declare that he was president of Southeastern Oil Company.
4. He reported a monthly expenditure for rent of $1325 when his actual monthly rent was $2650.
5. He reported that he earned $12,500 in income in 1991 when in fact he received in excess of $30,000 in income.

This case offered the opportunity to apply the linguistic tools of conversational cooperation, semantics, communicative context, and language clues relevant to the identification of possible deception.

THE COOPERATIVE PRINCIPLE

This case produced a classic example of the prosecution's failure to apply Grice's maxims of conversational cooperation. Whether the event is an oral hearing or a written report, Grice's maxims (1975), as noted earlier, are relevant:

1. Be informative: say as much as necessary and no more.
2. Be sincere: say what is true.
3. Be relevant to the topic.
4. Be orderly, clear, and unambiguous

Count 1 of his indictment charged Bolles with failing to mention on his Form 6B that he held a brokerage account with Prudential Bache. After his indictment for perjury, Bolles said that it didn't seem relevant because he had never done anything with this account and, as a result, he had received no income from it. Even from the government's perspective, this kind of omission might well be thought to be either an unintentional oversight or due to his confusion about what the form really intended. From Bolles's perspective, it was simply not relevant information about his financial condition, which was what he thought the form wanted (his schema). In any case, this omission seems to be a questionable basis for a serious perjury charge. Interestingly, he was never even asked about this during his hearing.

Count 2 charged that on his Form 6B Bolles made no mention of making lease payments on a Jaguar automobile. At the October 31 hearing, the transcript records:

> Creditor: Ah, this claim regarding, uh, I believe it's a Porsche, is that right? Uh, have you made demand on the bank or this Bill Parisi?
> (skip conversation upon Agent's request)

If Bolles answered this question we will never know, because at this point in the hearing the FBI agent intervened to stop any discussion of it. A logical reason it was skipped is that an investigator had meanwhile discovered that this lease was held by another person. In fact, it even had expired. Clearly, Bolles had followed Grice's maxim of relevance here. Once the government discovered this information, it became at best questionable to preserve it as count 2 in his indictment.

As for count 3, it is absolutely true that on his Form 6B Bolles did not declare that he was president of South East Oil. The first question on the form asked: "Income from employment or operation of business," to which Bolles wrote: "South East Oil Co., $12,500.00 1/1/91–9/26/91." He had answered exactly what the question asked, namely the amount of income he made from his employment or operation of business. Nowhere was he asked what his position in that company was. But even though Bolles did not identify himself as president of the company on his Form 6B, this role was clarified completely in the hearing of October 31:

Creditor: What do you do for South East?
A: I'm actually the current president of the company.

Then later in the same hearing Bolles repeated this information:

Creditor: What is your compensation arrangement with the company?
A: Um, well, what I've been doing has been getting, uh, around two thousand a month and then reimbursing with expenses at direct expense reimbursement.
Creditor: As the president?
A: As the president. Right now the company has no money.

We learn more about his income from this fledgling company later in the interview:

Creditor: Have you taken or received any money in connection with oil and gas production packages in the last two years?
A: Well, I've derived some income from selling some interest in oil and gas packages... That's the only way the company makes income...it has a negative net worth and if something doesn't change pretty quickly, it's gonna have a bankruptcy... Money came to the company and I was paid a salary, fee...that's basically two thousand dollars that I received.

There are times when it is difficult to understand why indictments include certain counts. If the prosecutor had looked carefully at his transcript of the October hearing, it should have been obvious to him that count 3 of the perjury charge was questionable. The 6B Form asked only what he earned. It did not ask if he was president of the company. In responding to this form, Bolles followed Grice's maxim of informativeness: South East Oil was a one-man operation, primarily trying to get gas and oil package contracts. When Bolles filled out Form 6B, he apparently didn't think it made any difference that he was president of this company, because the question asked only, "Income from employment or operation of business." In the subsequent hearing he volunteered twice that he was president when the questioners asked about the company. It seems hard to find any perjury here. The point of bankruptcy hearings, among other things, is to probe the answers given on Form 6B. That's exactly what the questioners did and it's exactly what Bolles answered.

Concerning count 4, on his Form 6B Bolles indicated that his monthly rent was $1325. At the 341 hearing, Bolles was questioned about this:

Receiver: How have you provided for living expenses during the period of time from the date of the receivership to the present?

A: I've lived with my girlfriend and then my wife and loans and gifts from my family.

The questioners did not probe this further, but if they had done so, it would have been apparent that the amount of the rent that Bolles reported was exactly half of what their investigators had discovered to be the true rent of the apartment, $2650. It does not take much investigative skill to figure out that if Bolles was living with his girlfriend, he was likely to be splitting half of the rent cost with her and that this amount was what he considered his expenditure for rent. At a minimum, they could have asked him about this. He was apparently following the maxims of relevance, informativeness, and sincerity here.

Of these four perjury counts, it is not difficult to see that two of them point either to Bolles's misunderstanding of the form's intent or to the way its questions were worded. The third count (about the automobile) was obviously the result of an intelligence gathering error and the fourth count was a simple matter of the government's failure to do the mathematics and probe more deeply. This left count 5 for further linguistic analysis. Bolles's lawyer asked me for help on this count in particular.

THE MEANING OF "INCOME"

Count 5 claimed that Bolles deliberately misrepresented his yearly income on his 6B schedule where he filled in the blank space indicating that his income was $12,500 a year. Since the questioners were not too sure about this, they asked about it in his October 31 hearing:

Receiver: Mr. Boles, you are aware that I was appointed your receiver on October the tenth, 1989 or thereabouts and since that time have you had any income from any source?

A: Yes, I have had income.

Receiver: What has been the source of your income?

A: Uh, salary.

Receiver: Okay, what has been the total amount of your income since October the tenth, 1989 to the present?

A: The total income? Probably about, I don't know what—

Creditor: Excuse me, his schedules list approximately two thousand dollars a month the last six months.

Receiver: My question is broader than that. My question is from the time of the date of the receivership to the present.

A: Probably about thirty-five thousand dollars.

Receiver: Okay, and what was done with those proceeds?

A: I maintained my, uh, household.

Receiver: Okay, did you have any income from any other source?

A: I did not.

Receiver: Okay, you're aware under the terms of the order that was entered in state court that any income of any source was to be turned over to me as your receiver?

A: No, I was not aware that I had to turn over the income mainly in the form of gifts.

Bolles's Lawyer: Was this thirty-five thousand dollars you're talking about income or in the form of gifts or—?

A: Mainly in the form of, uh, I don't know how you put it. It was mainly in the form of gifts, I guess, and some incomes that I made. I wasn't aware that I had to turn over uh, any monies to use for my living expenses.

Receiver: Okay, but the thirty-five thousand dollars, so the record is clear, that thirty-five thousand dollars was income that you earned?

The Court (ignoring the Receiver's question): Who did your income come from?

A: Well, my mother gave me money for living expenses.

Creditor: You know, when you classify it as income, you're talking about wages and—

Receiver: Exactly. Let me make sure you understand my question... When I say income, I mean money that's paid to you in connection with a job, not money that's given to you either as a loan or a gift.

A: I had, uh, I had income so far this year of twelve thousand five hundred dollars... My mother gave me fifteen thousand dollars for the bankruptcy retainer.

Receiver: Okay, so that leaves eight thousand dollars. Where'd the eight thousand dollars come from? Income that you've earned from a job?

A: Uh, I guess you can call it loans from friends, mainly.

Creditor: What he's asking you is what income from a job you have received. And your answer is the twelve thousand five hundred dollars?

A: That's my answer.

Receiver: So you had no other income than the twelve thousand dollars that's listed on your schedule?

A: That's correct.

It is possible from this exchange either that Bolles was uncertain or confused about the meaning of "income" or that he was dissembling. The questioners returned to this issue later in the hearing and Bolles stayed with his previously confusing answers:

Creditor: It was South East Oil Company that you did that for?

A: It was income from the company. Money came into the company and I was paid a salary, fee, whatever it was for that.

This exchange reveals a number of things. First of all, one would hope that a president of an oil company would have some idea about the meaning of "income." Was he faking incompetence here or was his confusion genuine? Bolles likely would be guilty of perjury unless his responses were the result of genuine ignorance or confusion about the meaning of "income." A skeleton view (the gist only) of the above-cited salient discussion about income is as follows:

Questioner	*Bolles*
1. Any income?	Yes
2. Source of income?	Salary
3. How much income to present?	Total income? I don't know what—
4. Schedule says $2000 a month	Probably about $35,000 (yearly)
5. Any income from other source?	Not aware I had to turn over gifts
6. Was $35,000 income or gifts?	Mainly gifts I guess
7. The $35,000 was earned income?	(Court's question blocks answer)
8. Who did income come from?	My mother gave me money
9. Income is wages, money paid for your job, not money given as a loan or gift.	I had income of $12,500. My mother gave me $15,000
10. That leaves $8,000. Was it income from a job?	I guess you call it loans from friends mostly.
11. From South East Oil?	I was paid a salary, fee, whatever it was for that.

Aside from the issue that one might never want to do business with a company president who is confused about the meaning of a normal business term like "income," the hearing officers had the difficult task of deciding whether Bolles was really that ignorant or whether he was just stringing them along.

In 2 above, Bolles equates "salary" with "income." That seems fair enough except that it was not really what the questioners were after here.

In 3, his certainty slips a little. He says, "I don't know what—" but we don't know how he would have finished his statement because he was interrupted by a follow-up question. It is possible, if not likely, that he was starting to say something like, "I don't know what you mean by income."

In 5, we learn that he was "not aware" that he had to report to his receiver the gifts that he got from others. This leads to 6, where he is asked if the $35,000 annual money was from income or gifts. Apparently not sure where this was going, he replied vaguely with a tagged on "I guess." In fact, he said "I guess" five other times during the hearing, along with other vague expressions such as "mainly," "mostly," and "basically."

It begins to look like they are all finally sharing the meaning of "income," until in 8 Bolles again defines income as gifts from his mother. Apparently he still didn't get the distinction they were trying so hard to make.

In 9, the questioner, perhaps exasperated, explained the difference between income and loans or gifts. Bolles appeared to understand this as he separated the $12,500 in income from the $15,000 in gifts.

In 10, the questioner explained that this still doesn't add up to the $35,000 per year that he had reported on his Form 6B. Bolles appeared to begin to understand that they have been at cross-purposes, adding sheepishly, "I guess," and "mostly" in his answer.

In 11, Bolles was still uncertain about what to call "income," equating "fee" with "salary" and referring to the questioner's previous definition as, "whatever you call it." It was their definition, of "income," but apparently still not his.

Linguistic signals of Bolles's semantic uncertainty and confusion abound here. In this brief colloquy Bolles said "I don't know what," "not aware," "I guess," "mainly," "mostly," and "whatever it was." Was he lying or simply inept?

THE MEANING OF "ASSETS"

If Bolles didn't understand what "income" meant, he was equally unsure about the meaning of "assets." On his 6B schedule, he was required to list all assets. His receiver asked about this as well:

Receiver: Now, as you know, there were certain assets that were turned over to me as your receiver. I noticed on your schedule that you list a lawsuit for thirty-five thousand dollars.

A: That, that is a lawsuit that hasn't been filed. It's just a potential claim that—(This part of the conversation skipped, upon Agent's request)

Again, we can't know what this is all about because the FBI agent who was present at the hearing requested that it be omitted. We can hypothesize, however, that either Bolles had listed the *potential* receipts from a lawsuit he was planning to bring against somebody else or, less likely, that somebody else was planning to bring a lawsuit against him and somehow he conceived of this as an asset. Both alternatives fail semantically to be considered an asset. If somebody were about to sue Bolles, it would be a liability. If Bolles were suing somebody else, it would be ludicrous to call it an asset, especially when the lawsuit had not even been filed. The most we can conclude from this is that, like "income," Bolles had little or no idea about the meaning of "asset."

CONTEXT AND POSSIBLE DECEPTION

To determine whether Bolles was being deceptive here, we have to take into account the contextual features that are central to the deceptive situation. So what contextual evidence can we find that Bolles was or was not lying? The good intelligence analyst notices contextual clues.

The first contextual clue is that we know he is likely to be a pretty bad businessman or he wouldn't be in bankruptcy court in the first place. Secondly, although it is not practical to produce all of the 6B schedule and hearing transcript here, it showed elsewhere that he had run up of hundreds of thousands of dollars in debts and had borrowed huge sums of money from his mother, among other people.

As for language clues, one can consider his constantly inept way of speaking, including but not limited to the ineptness revealed in the passages cited above. In addition to his apparent confusion about "income" and "assets," he requests clarification of the meaning of words like "presents." When asked about gifts, he says: "Mainly in the form of, uh, you know, I don't know how you put it. It was mainly in the form of gifts I guess and some incomes that I made." Later he says, "I guess you can call it loans from friends mainly." Still later he says, "I, uh, you know, I don't know what the figures, you're asking me something that I'm not real sure how to answer." He is not even clear about when he became president of South East Oil: "somewhere in that period." He's not sure whether his wife acquired interest in the company before his marriage or after: "I don't, I can't remember if it was before. I think it may have been before our marriage. I'm not sure." At one point, after some vigorous questioning, Bolles was even unsure about the speech event that he was in: "This isn't a trial I don't think, is it?"

As Galasinski observes, "it is impossible to find out empirically whether a speaker did or did not attempt to be deceptive" (114). All we can rely upon are clues to deception. These contextual clues suggest that Bolles was not being deceptive about his incompetence. His life experiences and his use of language showed it clearly. On the other hand, the hallmark of deceptive speakers is their inconsistencies. When we find inconsistent representations, we have either a very unskilled liar or a person who understands the questions differently, who understands the meanings of words in different ways, or who simply has a poor memory. Ekman's checklist of lies (1985, Table 4) lists thirty-eight clues to deception, including whether the person is practiced in lying, inventive and clever with his lies, has a good memory, and is a smooth talker with a convincing manner (291). Bolles displayed none of these characteristics.

If Bolles was lying, he was very inconsistent in pulling it off. His first inconsistency was that he reported an annual income of $35,000 on his 6B schedule, then later recorded it as $12,500. Was he the typically inconsistent liar or a bumbling businessman? Supporting the latter is evidence that he did not understand the intention of the form. Perhaps the most serious problem, as the hearing revealed, was that Bolles showed no clear understanding of what "income" and "assets" really mean, illustrated by his confusion and admitted ignorance of what was wanted of him.

Another important aspect of deception is that the speakers make a deliberate effort to communicate false information. A perceptive liar would not be likely to make the mistake of filling out the 6B Statement of Affairs with internally conflicting information, as Bolles clearly did. In contrast, human communication often includes factual errors about which the speaker is unaware. He was either very bad at lying or a very incompetent businessman. But it's hard to imagine that an inept and confused businessman like Bolles was incapable of making factual errors. He had apparently made enough such errors to find himself in his present situation of bankruptcy.

(4)
False statements in a political contribution conduit scheme

From August 1994 to December 1996, the government investigated fraud, false statements, and illegal campaign contributions in Pennsylvania. Based on the belief that certain corporations were violating the Federal Election Campaign Act, Title 2, U.S. Code 442b(a), the government targeted Empire Sanitary Landfill. Empire's officials were suspected of conspiring and then making corporate contributions in the name of third persons during the election campaigns of various nationally known politicians. At that time, laws prohibited corporations from making contributions or expenditures in connection with the nomination and election of candidates for federal office, and they also prohibited any officer of a corporation from contributing to candidates for federal office.

The government believed that the Empire officers had identified candidates that they wanted to support, had solicited campaign contributions from third parties, including employees, business associates, family, and friends, and had used them as "conduits" (also called "straw donors") by promising them that the company would reimburse their campaign contributions with corporate funds. Empire allegedly used corporate money to reimburse these donors for their contributions, disguising the corporation's books to make the reimbursements appear to be entertainment expenses. Empire's officers allegedly used these conduits for their company's contributions, reporting false information to the Federal Election Committee. The government believed that some $129,000 passed through Empire's conduit scheme to various political campaign committees that accepted these contributions, including the Dole for President Committee, the Clinton/Gore Campaign Committee, the Arlen Specter Presidential Exploratory Committee, the Rick Santorum Committee, the Friends of Max Baucus, and a few others.

In October 1997, the United States District Attorney for the Middle District of Pennsylvania issued a 139-count indictment of five Empire officers and one count against state Representative Frank Serafini (3 CR-97–225). One of the checks in evidence was for $2000 that an Empire officer had sent to Serafini. The government believed it was to repay him and his legislative aid for their previous $1000 contributions to the political campaign of Robert Dole for President. Complicating matters, the check from Empire was signed by Serafini's nephew, Michael Serafini, who was the assistant secretary of Empire and at the same time chairman of the New Jersey steering committee to elect Robert Dole as president.

The government further claimed after Empire had heard that an investigation was in progress and, before the indictments were made, the company's officers called a meeting and provided certain employees with company-constructed letters stating that their contributions went directly to various political campaigns rather than going through Empire's alleged conduit scheme. The company instructed some of its employees, the government believed, to submit phony invoices to the company to cover their contributions as legitimate company expenses.

Grand jury investigations about this matter began in April 1997. Based on their testimony, five of Empire's officers were indicted on charges of perjury and fraud. When the grand jury met a second time in September 1997, Representative Frank Serafini was called to testify, ultimately leading to the last count in the indictment, count 140, alleging his role in this conduit scheme. The $2000 check mentioned above was the centerpiece of Serafini's indictment. The government claimed that $1000 of this check, sent by Empire's Michael Serafini, was a conduit reimbursement to his uncle, Frank Serafini, for his contribution to the Dole campaign. The other $1000 was a conduit reimbursement that Serafini was supposed to pass along to his former legislative aide, who had also made a $1000 contribution to the Dole campaign.

After Frank Serafini was indicted, his attorney called me to provide a linguistic analysis of his grand jury testimony that led to his charge of perjury. My task was to determine the extent to which the language used by the prosecutor and Serafini during his grand jury appearance was clear and precise or whether, in at least some instances, the language was imprecise and suggested the possibility of multiple interpretations.

THE MEANING OF "REIMBURSE"

Several times during his testimony, Serfini insisted that the check for $2000 was not a reimbursement for his own and his administrative assistant's contributions to the Dole campaign. The way the prosecutor and Serafini used the word "reimburse" was at the center of this dispute and is emphasized below:

Q: And did you bring the documents pursuant to the subpoena that required your appearance today?

A: The way I read the subpoena is . . . "all the documents relative to political contributions you were *reimbursed* for." And I was not *reimbursed* for any contributions.

Q: Well then why wouldn't he [Michael Serafini] *reimburse* you for your Dole contribution?

A: Because I wanted to contribute to Bob Dole.

As the prosecutor questioned him further, Serafini explained that his nephew, Michael Serafini, an Empire business official who also headed the local campaign fund for Bob Dole, lived with him and often needed money for various things, recently including money to fix his automobile. His nephew had paid the $2000 back to him for previous money that Frank Serafini had advanced to him to pay for car repairs. Serfini then described how his large, close family worked:

A: We frequently transfer money between ourselves. I would have assumed that this was for the repair of an automobile or something... as I recall, I was fixing his car, his transmission went in his car. I had his car repaired...

Q: Was it a direct *reimbursement* for your Dole contribution?

A: Absolutely not in my mind. I don't have to be *reimbursed* for that contribution. I gave to Bob Dole because I like Bob Dole... this was not a *reimbursement* in my mind. It just wasn't.

The prosecutor then showed Serafini a stack of about fifty consecutively numbered checks for $2,000 from Empire to various employees, all of which were signed by his nephew, with Serafini's check in the stack. Serafini continued to testify that he believed that this check was a repayment from his nephew for money Serafini had given him to get his car repaired. He personally had given $1000 to the Bob Dole campaign in a separate check:

Q: So you are saying you don't know what the other thousand dollars is for?

A: I would not relate it to that, not in my mind.

Q: What would you relate it for?

A: To something else, whether it was fixing his car, whether it was something else.

Not surprisingly, the prosecutor did not believe Serafini, as his indictment eventually indicated:

> The testimony of Frank Serafini, as he then and there well knew and believed, was false in that Defendant Michael Serafini issued a check dated April 25, 1995, payable to Frank Serafini in the amount of $2,000 which *reimbursed* Frank Serafini for his $1,000 contribution to the Dole Committee and also *reimbursed* him for the expense of *reimbursing* Thomas Harrison, his former legislative aid, $1,000 for a contribution Thomas Harrison made to the Dole Committee in the amount of $1,000 which was solicited by Frank Serafini and *reimbursed* by Frank Serafini.

The prosecutor also asked Serafini if he knew about other people who were allegedly reimbursed for their campaign contributions to Dole, including Serafini's father. To this question, Serafini answered:

> My impression was that my father was not *reimbursed*... None of us believe that we have to be *reimbursed* for Bob Dole's contribution.

My linguistic analysis of Frank Serafini's grand jury testimony began with an analysis of the speech act of reimbursement.

THE REIMBURSEMENT SPEECH ACT

The reimbursement speech act has a certain basic structure that must be realized if the event is to be considered felicitous and complete:

> A pays B some amount of money for X.
> B returns the payment to A for what A had paid to B for X.

As straightforward and simple as this appears, there are additional conditions that have to be met for the reimbursement act to be considered felicitous and complete:

1. B's return payment to A cannot be understood as a symbolic token of appreciation, as when a watch is presented at a retirement ceremony or a plaque given for outstanding service.
2. B's return payment to A cannot be understood as a gift that is unrelated to any compensation for A's past payment for X.
3. B's return payment to A has to be understood by B to be directly associated with A's original payment for X.
4. A's receipt of B's return payment has to be understood by A to be directly related to A's original payment for X.

Unless there is mutual understanding about the reimbursement act, it cannot be defined as a reimbursement. Without such mutual understandings, the reimbursement act is not felicitous or complete. A true reimbursement act requires a meeting of the minds of both parties about the direct association of the repayment to the original payment. To accomplish these requirements, B can verify his understanding by stating the terms, reasons, or conditions of this repayment to A or A can verify how B's repayment to A was directly associated with A's original payment for X. Unless these terms are in writing or unless witnesses can vouch for the transaction, verification that a reimbursement occurred can be difficult to prove.

In perjury cases, the prosecutor needs to have factual evidence to compare with the language evidence used by the defendant. In this case, the prosecutor had no verifiable factual evidence that associated the $2,000 check Serafini received from his nephew Michael to directly connect it with Serafini's campaign contribution to the Dole campaign (conditions 1 and 3 above). In his grand jury testimony, Serafini denied this connection several times. The prosecutor also had no verifiable evidence to show that the $2000 check was directly associated with the Dole campaign (conditions 2 and 4 above). Nor could the prosecutor produce third party witnesses to verify a mutual understanding between the parties about this alleged payback. His only factual evidence was inferential, based on the fact that Sefarini's check came to the total of two campaign contributions and was nested among about fifty other checks issued by Empire for the same amount of money. Apparently that, along with the verifiable and admitted fact that Empire was paying for Serafini's current legal expenses in this matter, looked like enough to enable the prosecutor to infer Sefafini's guilt and to bring an indictment against him for perjury. Since his evidence was largely inferential, he needed to get convincing language evidence from Serafini's grand jury testimony to support it.

The prosecutor's next topic explored why Empire would agree to pay Serafini's legal expenses relating to grand jury appearance. His answer:

> You would have to ask them, it is very nice of them... They have been very nice to us... I didn't think I would need an attorney, to be very honest with you. I still don't.

When it came their turn to ask Serafini questions, members of the grand jury pursued the reimbursement issue again, but his response was consistently the same: "In my mind I was not reimbursed."

I decided to focus on three aspects of Serafini's grand jury testimony: the lack of a meeting of the minds about the meaning of "reimbursement," any language clues that might illuminate Serafini's intentions, and the prosecutor's unclear questioning technique.

THE LACK OF MUTUAL UNDERSTANDING

Before trial, the court denied Serafini's motion to dismiss the case, which was based on his attorney's claim that the prosecutor was unclear in his questions. In denying this motion, the Court said that the prosecutor's failure to define "reimbursement" did not warrant dismissal, although it would be up to the trial jury to determine this. The Court also left it up to the government to convince the jury that when Serafini said, "in my mind I was not reimbursed," this statement indicated that he knew that the $2000 check from Michael Serafini was a payback for his contribution to Dole, whether or not he thought of it as one in his own mind.

My examination of Serafini's grand jury testimony revealed that the prosecutor and Serafini used and understood the verb "reimburse" in different ways. Note what case law says about this:

> To sustain a perjury charge, prosecutor must present careful questioning in order to demonstrate that the defendant was aware of the meaning of the question and the falsity of the answer. For grand jury testimony to support a perjury charge, the meaning of prosecutor's question must be clear, and a court may not assume a particular meaning. An indictment must evidence a meeting of the minds of prosecutor, defendant, and grand jury in order to properly charge defendant with perjury for his grand jury statement.
> (*U.S. v. Serafini*, 7 F. Supp. 2d. 529, 537 (H.D. PA. 1998)).

The linguistic task was to examine how the two participants used and understood the meaning of "reimburse" throughout their exchanges. Perhaps thinking that everyone already knows what it means, the prosecutor did not define it. But throughout his testimony, Serafini gave clues about what he understood and meant by this term. For example, early in his questioning, the prosecutor asked Serafini about a partnership agreement with Empire that his father had set up when he sold his landfill company to Empire and made Serafini and his sister partners in that new agreement. He questioned Serafini about what income the partners were to receive from Empire for this. In his response, Serafini used "reimbursed" to indicate that as a partner, he would be paid a small percentage per ton of what the company earned for the disposal of waste in the landfill. There is no way that it could mean that Serafini first paid for something and then got it back as a reimbursement. He used the word "reimbursed" to describe what can be understood as his due compensation or pay:

> Serafini: Well, my understanding of the agreement...was that I have 50 percent, and my sister was given 50 percent...for waste that is disposed of in the landfill, for which we get reimbursed. My father distributes these funds.

And later, when the prosecutor asked Serafini about how his legal fees were being paid. Serafini responded:

> All I know is it was a fee agreement for a certain amount, of which I don't remember, and it was supposed to be reimbursed by Empire.

In both of these examples, Serafini clearly used "reimburse" to mean, "obligatory payment due according to contract, or to pay." This clearly was not the meaning that the prosecutor used and understood for this word.

When the judge denied Serafini's motion to dismiss the case, he also cited only one of the two glosses of "reimburse" in *Merriam-Webster's Collegiate Dictionary*: "**to pay back** an equivalent for something taken lost, or expended." He did not cite the second gloss, "to make restoration or payment of an equivalent to. Synonym: see **pay**." The Court's selection of only one of the definitions of "reimbursement" here opened the door for the prosecutor to indict Serafini based on the first part of the dictionary entry, "to pay back," meaning repayment for an initial payment made, rather than the way Serafini had used the word to indicate "to pay *for* goods or services."

It's unfortunate that the English language contains the verb "reimburse" to cover both of the glosses noted above, but even the most commonly used general dictionaries do not include the predictable corresponding verb, "imburse." If English had such a verb, things might have been clearer, for then "imburse" would clearly denote "pay" while "reimburse" would clearly mean "return pay" or "pay back." The common pattern of English is for a verb to have a given meaning without any prefixes or suffixes and to have an extended (or different) meaning by adding prefixes such as un- or dis- or, in this case, re-. It also would have been clearer if the prosecutor had simply used the expression, "pay back" instead of "reimburse," to make his meaning clearer. He apparently didn't notice that Serafini had been using a different meaning of this word. Both men used semantically different and therefore opposite glosses of the same dictionary entry, producing their different understandings about what they meant by the word.

REQUESTING CLARIFICATION

When there is a possibility of meanings that are misunderstood, vague, or ambiguous, recall that the U.S. Supreme Court decision in *Bronston* said that it is the prosecutor's job to clarify such things. After Serafini answered each question about "reimbursement," the prosecutor assumed that they meant the same thing, then changed the subject immediately, and moved on to ask his following questions on different topics. This is not to say that the prosecutor did this deliberately or employed a "hit-and-run" strategy, which has been known to occur in undercover investigations (Shuy 2005, 21–22). In all likelihood, the prosecutor and the judge were just as unaware of the different meanings of this word as Serafini was. They all apparently assumed that they had reached a meeting of the minds about the meaning of "reimburse."

Throughout the seventeen times that the prosecutor brought up "reimbursement," Serafini was consistent with his own "non-payback" definition in ten of these. When he finally seemed to begin to understand that the prosecutor meant "payback," he vehemently denied this in all five answers. On two occasions the prosecutor gave evidence of being confused by Serafini's responses when he indicated that he meant "pay for" rather than "pay back," but in neither of these times did the prosecutor request clarification about what Serafini meant by the word. There appeared to be no meeting of the minds here about the meaning of "reimburse" and no effort by either party to try to clarify something that neither perceived to be a problem.

This was not the first time "reimburse" became an issue in the courts. In response to Serafini's motion to dismiss, the Court cited the Third Circuit's conclusion in another case relevant to the issue of ambiguity of the word, "reimburse," which concluded, "there is nothing ambiguous in the question or the answer":

> That the prosecutor and defendant understood each other is evidenced by the defendant's unequivocal denials that their behavior merited the labels in question. At no time in the course of their testimony did the defendants manifest the slightest uncertainty or confusion as to the meaning of these terms. Indeed, the defendants themselves used the terms in their vehement denials. The record reveals a meeting of the minds on the definition of the words. (Long, 534 F.2d at 1100)

Two points are noteworthy in the Third Circuit's opinion. The first is that this Court also cited only one of the standard dictionary definitions of "reimburse," "to pay back (an equivalent for something taken, lost, or expended) to someone," but ignored the other gloss, "to pay for," adding in the denial of the motion to dismiss: "The words used were to be understood in their common sense, not as they might be warped by sophistry or twisted in pilpul." But what is the "common sense" of "reimburse" when two common sense meanings are listed even in commonly used general dictionaries? Is lexicographic analysis of this word mere sophistry? Still, the Third Circuit's opinion was consistent with that of the Serafini Court, which concluded: "it is reasonable to conclude that Mr. Serafini understood that the prosecutor wanted to know whether defendant Frank Serafini had been reimburse*d* for...the Dole contribution." To be consistent with case law is perhaps a good thing, but not so good when it flies in the face of at least potentially confusing usage.

The second noteworthy point is that the Third Circuit Court put the onus on the defendant for not clarifying this matter, saying that he should have manifested some uncertainty or confusion, but did not do so. This is a bit surprising, because legal precedent states clearly that it is the questioner's burden, not the defendant's, to be certain that the terms being used are clear and unambiguous. If Serafini thought he understood the prosecutor to be using "reimbursement" to mean "pay for" rather than "pay back," the prosecutor had seventeen opportunities to disabuse him of this notion. He did not do so. As noted earlier, this is not to say that the prosecutor was deliberately trying to trick Serafini. It's more likely that neither he nor the courts had even considered the two meanings of this word. Other courts have ruled that words such as "dealings," "business dealings," "bribes," "kickbacks," and "payoffs" are sufficiently clear and definite to support a perjury indictment, because there can be little question about their intended meanings. In this case, "reimbursement" seemed to fall into this same category.

The Third Circuit Court also ruled that when a defendant vehemently denies an accusation, this is clear evidence that he understands the meaning. This is certainly true when the prosecutor and defendant have a mutual understanding (meeting of the minds) about the meaning of the terms being used. In the Serafini case, the language of both men over the entire hearing shows that such a mutual understanding was far from evident. Once it appeared that he was beginning to think he might be understanding what the prosecutor was getting at, Serafini vehemently denied that his $2000 check was a payback for his Dole contribution.

INTENTIONALITY

One of the criteria used to determine perjury is that the defendant was aware of the meaning of the question and the falsity of his answer. When the Court ruled against Serafini's motion to dismiss, it also focused on Serafini's repeated claim when he said that he "did not believe in my mind" that he had received reimbursements for his contributions to Dole.

But the Court ruled that at trial the prosecution would have to bear the burden of demonstrating that Serafini knew and believed that the check he received was a reimbursement, adding that every perjury charge requires proof that the defendant knowingly made a false statement under oath. The prosecutor used a verbal variant of this in his indictment: "he then and there well knew and believed." Tiersma points out that the word "knowingly" has spawned endless litigation because its scope is virtually always ambiguous (Tiersma 1999, 60–61). Grammatically, "knew and believed" are verbs that modify the sentence predicate "made false statements under oath." The problem with both the verbal "knew and believed" and adverbial "knowingly" is that they both claim to reach into the mind of the accused, which task requires evidence that is virtually impossible to prove and which many counter-examples of their use can illustrate. For example, if people who keep kosher happen to eat foods that they think are kosher but actually contain pork, they could not be said to have acted "knowingly" or have "known and believed" they had eaten pork.

As noted earlier, it's not possible for any science, including linguistics, to reach into a person's mind to discover intentions. Prosecutors are no exception. In this case, Serafini said several times that "in my mind" (indicating that he believed it) the $2000 check from his nephew was to pay him back for money that he had advanced to repair his nephew's car. The prosecutor's questions about this did not cause Serafini to change his statements, knowledge, or belief. At trial, the prosecution had to prove that Serafini's "in my mind" was not true, a monumental task, especially while the two men were implicitly defining and using the key term, "reimburse," very differently. Since the definition of "reimburse" was never clarified, there was no way that the prosecutor could prove that Serafini knew and believed the check was a part of Empire's conduit scheme.

In language exchanges of extreme importance, such as grand jury questions and answers, the needs to follow the maxims of the cooperative principle (Grice 1975) and to request clarification about unclear matters are magnified. The burden is on the person in control, the one who has the power to manage the exchanges so that there will be no residual ambiguity. It is up to the superordinate speaker to use vocabulary, syntax, logical discourse sequence, and referencing clearly to the subordinate speaker and to clarify any ambiguity that occurs.

SYNTAX CLARITY

Words and intentions were not the only evidence of faulty communication in this prosecution. Although both speakers used "reimburse" with different referential meanings, the prosecutor's syntax was also far from clear. His eleventh question, for example, contained two parallel clauses, two subordinate "that" clauses, and eight levels of clausal and phrasal embedding. His twelfth question, seventy-eight words long, contained three parallel structures (the second producing an ungrammatical run-on sentence), eight prepositional phrases, three "that" clauses, and fifteen levels of clausal and phrasal embedding.

Suspecting that the prosecutor may have been selective in his use of complex syntax to different witnesses in the same grand jury hearing, I compared his broad syntax patterns in the most crucial area of Serafini's testimony with the testimony of one of the other defendants in this case, Robert Giglio, and found:

This comparison shows that this same prosecutor was quite capable of asking short, direct, and syntactically clear questions, that he was capable of requesting clarification about potential suspected ambiguity, and that he was capable of asking questions that contain few embedded clauses and phrases. The unanswered question here is why

	To Giglio	*To Serafini*
Average words per sentence	9.6	21.6
Requests for clarification	4	0
Questions with three or more clauses	10%	46%
Questions with only one main clause	60%	38%

this prosecutor chose to use simpler and clearer sentence structures to a different witness in the same case.

Perjury law says: "Jury in a perjury prosecution cannot be allowed to speculate on (1) the prosecutor's meaning, (2) the defendant's meaning, and (3) the grand jury's meaning, with respect to grand jury questioning giving rise to the charge." Speech act, semantic, syntactic, and ambiguity analyses of the evidence in this case provided a different view of the case from that of the prosecutor. Speculation by the prosecutor, the defendant, and the courts seem to have been allowable here.

(5)
False statements and fraud in a bank loan

Defendants who are charged with making false statements often have considerably more legal problems than that. The more serious crime is commonly a fraud case in which the defendant made false statements. This was Larry Kopp's story, because he was charged with both fraud and perjury. It was fairly clear that he had committed fraud, but the charge of perjury was considerably less evident.

In the early 1980s, Larry Kopp and his brother, Marvin Kopp, started a real estate development business in New Jersey that they operated through various corporations and partnerships. After Marvin died in 1984, the business fell on hard times financially and disputes arose among Larry, his brother's widow, Judith, and her son, David. By the spring of 1987, David Kopp had become the managing partner, while his uncle, Larry Kopp, continued to be involved. Meanwhile the company's business and finance problems grew worse and worse.

They tried hard to right the ship, and in August 1987 the Kopp partnership began to negotiate with Ensign Bank for a $13 million dollar second mortgage loan, most of which was to be used to help finance a shopping mall that the partnership owned. The first lenders soon learned about this second mortgage and were about to declare a default on their own loan to the Kopps. To ward this off, the Kopp's office manager, Stuart Sherer, created and forged signatures on false leases that inflated the true amount of rental income that the shopping mall was generating. This documentation falsely indicated that the mall was fully occupied and that its rental stream would be enough to cover the mortgage payments on their new loan from Ensign Bank.

Ensign Bank relied on these false representations and loaned the Kopp partnership $13 million. Even with this additional funding, the partnership could not recover financially and about a year later was forced into default on their Ensign mortgage. Larry Kopp blamed this mess on his nephew David's diversion of partnership money and failure to collect the rent. The bank demanded and received the deed in lieu of foreclosure and eventually sold the property for $14.5 million, claiming that the transaction actually lost them $3.4 million because of lost interest, operating expenses for taking over the property, and the cost of a low-interest loan to the new buyer.

Federal authorities had discovered the fraud in May 1988, when David Kopp admitted his complicity and agreed to cooperate in the prosecution of Stuart Sherer and David's uncle, Larry Kopp. David then began tape-recording his conversations with other alleged conspirators, including one recorded conversation with his uncle Larry, which the agents did not find very helpful to Larry's prosecution.

Still believing that Larry Kopp was deeply involved in the fraudulent inducement to get the bank loan from Ensign, the government decided to use its common and effective strategy of beginning the investigation of Larry Kopp with a lower level person in the company, office manager Sherer. This strategy often yields useful information about how to get evidence on the higher level actors. When a government agent confronted Sherer about this matter, he confessed his role in the scheme, but told them that his boss, Larry Kopp, had instructed him to commit the fraud. The government then offered Sherer certain considerations for helping them in the investigation in exchange for his tape-recording conversations with Larry Kopp, hoping that forthcoming tape-recorded evidence would verify the accusations made by both David Kopp and Sherer about Larry Kopp's alleged role in the false report of the mall's rental income.

UNDERCOVER CONVERSATIONAL STRATEGIES

The prosecutor wanted to discover whether Larry Kopp instigated the fraud or was at least aware it and subsequently issued false statements about it. Based on the admissions of David Kopp and Sherer, the government knew that fraud and forgery had taken place. The issue at trial was to prove that Larry Kopp was responsible for it. The factual evidence gathered in this fraud case was not an issue that linguistics could help resolve, but Larry Kopp's defense lawyer asked me to analyze four covertly tape-recorded conversations with Kopp to see whether perjury charges against him could stand up. These recordings were made over a period of three months before Ensign Bank foreclosed in late 1988.

It is likely that government agents coached Sherer before he started his covert taping. In undercover operations like this, the person wearing the microphone is usually instructed to follow a four-step sequential procedure (Shuy 2005, 7–9):

1. First let the subject talk. If he implicates himself clearly, stop. If not, go to the next step.
2. Drop hints or imply illegality. If the subject picks up on the hints and implicates himself, stop. If not, go to step 3.
3. Retell the past events that indicate guilt. If the subject agrees with the retelling, stop. If not, go to step 4.
4. Be clear and unambiguous about all aspects of the guilt. If the subject agrees, stop. If he disagrees, the case will be hard to make against him.

On the first tape (August 8, 1988), Sherer followed step 1 for about ten minutes, while they talked about house mortgages, losing a CD, and other company business, but Kopp said nothing incriminating. Sherer then began the hinting and retelling strategies (steps 2 and 3), suggesting the illegality of the Ensign Bank fraud and hoping that Kopp would take the bait and say something incriminating about his involvement. Kopp replied that if they had any potential legal problem, it would go away if they could only manage to sell the mall and repay the $13 million loan. He anticipated a civil suit if they couldn't do this, but he displayed no concerns about possible criminal charges. Sherer encouraged Kopp's belief that there would be no criminal investigation, even though, of course, Sherer was already caught in it.

The worst part of this conversation for Kopp was that he admitted that he knew that the shopping mall leases were phony. But he gave no indication about what Sherer was trying to get him to say—that he had instigated the scheme. His view of the matter was that his nephew David was responsible for the fraud because of his sloppy management. In the next few days, they were to have an important meeting with Ensign Bank about their financial problem, but Kopp seemed unconcerned about protecting himself and was more interested in protecting Sherer:

Sherer: Kind of skipping back to the Ensign…I feel a little exposed and hoping that you and I will work out the scenario so that we're protected.

L. Kopp: We're blaming everything on David. David's lack of paying attention, lack of response to them. His job was to supply all this paperwork. Make him the scapegoat. If they say, "What do you mean, you didn't know? You didn't ride by and take a look?" Say "I haven't ridden by there in months."

Sherer: Here's a copy of that sheet that you and I had gone over, showing all the estoppels and all the leases.

L. Kopp: When we go to that meeting, I'm not gonna wanna know any of this stuff. It's like the papers got stuck in front of me, so I signed 'em. But we're gonna blame it all on him. They were all turned over to David.

Sherer: Probably when you asked me to make up all the phony leases, we shoulda got David more intimately involved.

L. Kopp: Probably it would have been easier if he actually was. The fact is that they are there and that the things aren't for real. The only concern at this point is criminal, period. How can you prove that you did it or I did it or he did it? Things weren't on there, Nutra Systems, Off Limits... [names of businesses with leases at the shopping mall].

THE RECENCY PRINCIPLE

The government believed that when Sherer said, "Probably when *you asked me to make up all the phony leases,* we shoulda got David more intimately involved," Kopp seemed to be agreeing that he told Sherer to make up the phony leases. But notice that Sherer's statement contained two propositions: (1) a dependent clause, "when you asked me to make up the phony leases," and (2) a main clause, "we shoulda got David more intimately involved." Notice also that Kopp replied only to the second, the main clause, but not to Sherer's statement that Kopp was involved, which Sherer slipped into the first dependent clause. The recency principle that is often found in covert tape-recordings was at work here. "It is commonplace that when agents drop hints into the conversation and are unsure how their targets might react, they often quickly change the subject to something benign before they give up their turn of talk" (Shuy 2005, 22). This is particularly troublesome when the implication of guilt is not in the main part of the statement. The recency principle is aided not only by syntax, but also by phonetic stress and intonation. Main clauses at the ends of sentences, including Sherer's here, are frequently also slightly louder and more stressed.

PRONOUN AMBIGUITY

The pronoun references are also problematic when the "you" and "we" can refer to either the company or to the individuals being addressed, causing referential ambiguity. Sherer's ambiguous "you" in "when you asked me" could as easily refer to the company he worked for as to Kopp personally. The same can be said for his use of "we."

The conversation continued:

Sherer:	Well I know they're not looking to do anything criminal. Basically, you and I did—[short pause] but they'll never know that.
L. Kopp:	They could, but deep down I really don't think it's gonna even come up unless we can't sell the property.

Here Sherer comes close to following the undercover stage 4 unambiguous representation of illegality, but he pauses and stops short of it, using what researchers call the cloze procedure, where you provide part of a sentence and then let the listener fill in the blank part. Sherer paused briefly at that point and then tried to assure Kopp that the government really doesn't know about anything criminal going on. Again Kopp responds to the latter, most recent part of Sherer's statement ("but they'll never know that") but not to Sherer's unfinished sentence, "Basically, you and I did—." Kopp allows that the government could know something inexplicitly stated but "it" (ambiguous reference) is not likely to be a problem unless the company can't sell the shopping mall before they are foreclosed.

Sherer: Well, when I prepared those and you reviewed them, everything looked pretty good to you, didn't it?

L. Kopp: Yeah. It's a pissing contest. How could they prove that if it was or wasn't signed? I mean it wasn't signed. You didn't sign your name on it. They weren't even notarized. I really don't think that it's gonna be a problem unless we just can't sell it. We have to show good faith, that's really what they want.

Here Kopp's two uses of "it" are references to their $13 million loan that they were about to discuss in a meeting with Ensign Bank, when Kopp wanted to try to prevent the bank from foreclosing.

Sherer tape-recorded a second conversation with Kopp three days later, on August 11, still fishing for Kopp to say words that would incriminate himself. When the government agents find it necessary to make a second tape-recording, it's usually clear that they didn't get what they needed in the first one. Here Sherer took the same approach, asking for Kopp's advice about what to do and say to the investigators. Kopp remained firm that it was all David's fault, indicating that they learned about the fraud after the fact:

Sherer: I guess we should review what we are going to say and what we are not.

Kopp: It could be a criminal thing, if it comes up. Hey, we were as much in the dark as you about it. David Kopp was given all that stuff... and we only found out about it after it happened.

CONTRASTING AGENDAS

His second tape gave Sherer even less than he got on his first try. Still not completely satisfied, on August 30 the government had David Kopp make a phone call to his uncle Larry. This too yielded nothing useful to implicate Larry Kopp, because their topics were about various bids on the possible sale of the shopping mall and about their unpaid bills for insurance and taxes. If David Kopp was trying to catch his uncle in something incriminating, he did a poor job of fishing for it, and Larry Kopp said nothing that would implicate himself personally about instigating the fraud.

The government then sent Sherer back to tape-record still another conversation with Larry Kopp on September 16, 1988. Sherer used less trickery in his language, and the tape again yielded nothing that showed Kopp was responsible for creating the fraud. Their topics were about various leases in the shopping mall and several offers they had received to purchase it, none of which came close to showing Larry Kopp's instigation of the fraudulent scheme. They also talked about how to stall Ensign Bank from foreclosing their loan, but again nothing incriminating about Larry Kopp came out.

Thirty-six minutes into the conversation, Sherer finally introduced the topic of the fraudulent leases they gave to Ensign Bank. Sherer again was not specific enough to cause Kopp to consider that this topic was about a law enforcement investigation. His response was clearly about what Ensign Bank was thinking, not about the government:

Sherer: You know what I'm afraid of is obviously the estoppels and the leases.

Kopp: I believe they've kind of given up on that tack. I also believe that they convinced themselves that the property is really worth what they got in there and that they are gonna get out whole. They're a little anxious to see

> if they could steal it from me because if they get any more, then they get to keep the money. There have been no more threats at all as far as doing anything with that...

PRONOUN REFERENCING

Sensing that he was getting nowhere by simply hinting (step 2), Sherer then returned to the topic of blaming David:

> Sherer: Are we gonna stick with the same tack that David is the one who did everything?
>
> Kopp: I don't see any reason why not. Absolutely, absolutely.
>
> Sherer: I mean, otherwise we both go to jail for a long time. And I don't want any part of that.
>
> Kopp: No, we're in cahoots when it comes to that, obviously. I got to tell you that my gut feeling is that it doesn't enter into the picture. I will agree with you that if we sell it, we come out okay.

Sherer still had not managed to convince Kopp that they were in danger of criminal charges, and Kopp continued to believe that everything would work out just fine if they could sell the shopping mall before Ensign Bank foreclosed on them. Sherer's "otherwise we could both go to jail" was ambiguous, because even though he probably was referring to himself and Larry Kopp, his inclusive "we" could also refer to David Kopp and Sherer. When Larry Kopp agrees, "we're in cahoots when it comes to that," his agreement is that Sherer and David Kopp should not go to jail. Larry Kopp clearly knew that someone had committed fraud and he continues in his belief that the blame for this should fall on David Kopp, not on Sherer.

THE INDICTMENT

After the government covertly tape-recorded these four conversations with Larry Kopp over a period of two months, the prosecutor decided to bring an indictment of twelve counts of fraud and false statements against Kopp. In spite of the less-than-convincing evidence of the tapes, the first seven counts charged Kopp with fraudulent pretenses to secure permanent financing to replace the loan from Ensign Bank. Counts 8 to 11 charged him with submitting documents to the trust company that he signed, acting as attorney-in-fact for his sister-in-law, Judith Kopp, noting that he wasn't authorized to do so. Count 12 alleged that Kopp defrauded his tenants by overcharging them for their insurance and taxes.

I gave my topic analyses of the tapes to Kopp's defense attorney, showing contrastive agendas, information about pronoun-referencing ambiguity, and the recency principle, which he used in his briefs. The government's intelligence gathering problems were apparently clear to the judge who then severed counts 1 through 7 and count 12, all relating to Larry Kopp's involvement in perpetrating the fraud. But the judge did not excuse him from having knowledge that the fraud had been committed by Sherer and his nephew, David Kopp, and for producing false statements about the company's financial condition. Larry Kopp appeared to have admitted knowledge of the fraud after the fact, but even in the covert tape-recordings he never admitted that he initiated it. Kopp pleaded guilty to the remaining four charges of fraudulent misrepresentations.

This case is an example of how linguistic analysis can help reduce the unverified counts of initiating the fraud, but there was no way that it could change the facts about Larry Kopp's guilt of false representations. Linguists can only work with the data available.

(6)
False statements on a hunting license application

It's well known that the state of Montana is a great place to hunt elk, deer, and other game. Many people go there to hike, fish, ski, visit the national parks at Glacier or Yellowstone, or to simply enjoy the beautiful mountain scenery. Some summer visitors like the state so much that they purchase property to live there year-round. Others maintain two homes, one in Montana and another in a different state or country. This can pose a problem for state Fish Game and Hunting officials, because visitors who come from out of state are required to purchase special, more restricted big game hunting licenses than are Montana's full-time residents. Like most states, Montana has strict rules about how to meet the requirements for residency relating to such things as taxation, educational benefits, driver's licenses, fishing, and hunting. Once in a while, outsiders fill out their license applications fraudulently, setting them up for charges of making false statements.

In the spring of 2005, an anonymous caller, probably anxious to help protect the state from illegal hunters, informed the Fish Game and Hunting warden of Musselshell County that he believed a retired physician, Randolph Turpin, had been hunting and taking deer and elk illegally in that county. A subsequent investigation showed that Turpin had purchased non-resident hunting licenses prior to 2002, but resident licenses since that time, since by then he had purchased a home in Montana. Taxidermy records revealed that he hired a local taxidermist to mount two bull elks for him in 2003 and 2004. When the warden brought this up to him, Turpin admitted that he had purchased his first resident big game license in 2002, but six months previous to that time he had been living in Switzerland, possibly in violation of the state's 180-day residence requirement.

Suspecting something was amiss, state investigators obtained a warrant and searched Turpin's rural Montana home and confiscated forty pieces of evidence that they believed supported charges of residency fraud and hunting without a proper license. They confiscated dozens of photographs and various game mounts on the walls of Turpin's Montana home, and subsequently indicted him on four counts, one of them a felony charge for the possession and unlawfully taking more than 2,000 pounds of bull elk and buck mule deer (which the prosecution was subsequently unable to prove), along with a misdemeanor charge of hunting without a proper license (*State of Montana Fourteenth Judicial Court Musselshell County v. Raldolph A. Turpin Cause No. ec-06-23*). Three other counts in his indictment were misdemeanors, one of which was that he made a materially false statement on his hunting license application form at a time when he claimed to be a resident when the prosecution claimed he was not. It is this last count that frames this analysis, because by the time the case came to trial, the prosecutor had increased the charge from a misdemeanor to a felony. Turpin was currently serving on boards of various corporations, and rules that prohibit felons from holding such positions would become a huge problem for him. He likely would have been willing to pay fines for misdemeanor charges, but he certainly didn't want to be convicted of a felony. So he hired a lawyer and fought the charge.

In her motion to dismiss the felony perjury charge, Turpin's lawyer believed that the Montana statute is so vague about residency requirements that the law is both void on its face and as it applied to a particular circumstance. She believed that it did not make clear to ordinary people exactly what conduct is prohibited, thereby encouraging arbitrary and discriminatory law enforcement.

She also planned to attack the process by which Montana hunting licenses are awarded. For this reason, she retained me to examine the language of the required forms as they relate to the state statute.

This chapter is a bit different from the others in this book, because it describes the lawyer's processes of determining which defense strategies would be best supported by linguistic analysis and which ones she and I both thought might or might not be effective in this case. I had an opportunity, rather rare for an expert witness, to help the lawyer decide which defense strategy might work best. Throughout the two years leading up to the trial, four defense strategies were proposed and then rejected, for reasons that will be explained. This chapter describes these four potential strategies and why they were rejected before trial in favor of a fifth strategy, which the lawyer then used successfully at trial.

STRATEGY 1: ATTACK THE AMBIGUITY OF THE CONSERVATION FORM

In the first step for obtaining a hunting license, an applicant fills out and signs a declaration on what the state calls a Conservation form, which says in its entirety:

> I hereby declare that I have been a LEGAL resident of the state of Montana, as defined by MCA 87–2–102 for at least 180 consecutive days. All statements on this form are correct and true. I understand that if I subscribe to or make a false statement on this form, I am subject to criminal prosecution.

Prospective hunters can pick up this form at many Montana grocery stores, hardware stores, gun shops, and fishing tackle shops. One serious problem with this form is that most ordinary people, even ordinary Montanans, do not know what the law, MCA 87–1–102, specifies and requires. The noun phrase, "LEGAL resident," contains no immediately identifiable meaning from which the applicant can be able to understand or even infer the definition that the wording on the form implies. Therefore, when people are asked to declare that they are legal residents for at least 180 consecutive days, they are not told what this means, since "180 consecutive days" does not specify when these 180 days begin or end. Further, when the form asks the applicant to vouch for or, as it says, "subscribe to," the fact that "all statements on this form are correct and true," this wording can encourage the applicant to believe that all of the statements *on the printed form itself* are correct and true. So at even this first stage of applying for a hunting license the prospective hunter is required to sign a form that contains vague and unstated information containing words and expressions that are not clearly defined.

If enterprising applicants should happen to look up and read the Montana statute before they sign this Conservation form, they would find, as will be elaborated later, that the statute contains some specific behavioral requirements, but this statute presents these in such a bewildering sequence that an ordinary reader can be discouraged from processing them easily and effectively.

Our initial strategy, then, was to show the inadequacies of the language used in the Conservation form. Next, we examined the application form for a hunting license.

STRATEGY 2: ATTACK THE AMBIGUITY OF THE APPLICATION FORM

After applicants fill out the Conservation form, their next step is to fill out and sign the Montana Resident Deer, Elk, & Antelope Application form and send it to the state licensing office in Helena. In small print under the usual requirements of name, address, birthdates, is the following declaration in which the applicant is required to fill in the empty blank spaces and sign:

> I hearby declare that I have been a legal resident for at least 180 consecutive days___ years ___ months immediately prior to making application for this license and that I qualify for the 30 day military exception or Montana Job Corp Camp exemption (MCA 87–2–102). I declare all statements on this form are true and correct and that the undersigned hereby agrees to use the information on this form for the purpose of verifying residency according to Sec 87–2–102.

Oddly, the grammar of this declaration specifies the highly unlikely possibility that applicants actually are legal residents *and at the same time* qualify for the military or Job Corp Camp exemption, which combination is highly irrelevant to the vast majority of civilian license applicants who are not at the same time members of the military or the Job Corp. In addition, there are three ambiguities in this declaration: "immediately prior to," "MCA-87–2–102," and "all statements on this form are true and correct."

1. "immediately prior to"

This application form echoes the less-than-clear wording, "immediately prior to," which was derived from the state's statute. *Black's Law Dictionary* defines "immediately" in two ways:

> (1) within a reasonable time having due regard to the nature of circumstances in the case, and
> (2) not deferred by any period of time.

One way for the form to be explicit about what "immediately prior to" means would be for the form to replace the ambiguous word, "immediately," with a defined and explicit time period, such as "180 days contiguous to the date of this application." Similarly, this form also echoes the ambiguity of the statute when it uses the word, "consecutive days," which specifies neither the beginning nor ending dates of whatever time period "consecutive" is intended to convey. As this form stands, "consecutive" could be *any* 180 consecutive days in the preceding year rather than the most recent, last, or contiguous consecutive days before applying. Perhaps applicants could infer this meaning, but one would hope for explicitness rather than needing to rely on their inferencing skills.

2. "MCA-87–2–102"

Here the Application form has the same problem as the Conservation form. Citing the source of the needed information without saying what that source says may be an efficient way to shorten the form, but it communicates little or no practical information to the majority of applicants, who are not likely to have committed this statute to memory. It is true that applicants can look up the statute, but this is very unlikely to happen.

3. "all statements on this form are true and correct"

Eighty "statements" appear on this form, of which the vast majority were made by the person or persons who wrote it. Therefore, the noun phrase, "all statements," is potentially ambiguous because it conveys two or more meanings. No doubt the form intended this construction to refer to only the statements that the applicant fills in. Perhaps some or even most readers understand this, but its literal meaning has to include the statements made by the writer of the form, and there is no way that license applicants can vouch for the accuracy or truth of what the form's writer wrote. The simplest way to revise this would be to say, "All of the statements *that I have made* on this form are true and correct." Such a sentence would clarify the utterance meaning regardless of what the form's writer may have intended it to mean (Tiersma 1999, 124–25).

STRATEGY 3: ATTACK THE AMBIGUITY OF THE STATUTE

After analyzing the Conservation and Application forms, we examined the statute itself. The first four paragraphs of the statute outline the requirements and benefits accruing to members of the armed forces and their dependents. Since the vast majority of applicants are not members of the armed forces, those who are not so connected have to persevere to the middle part of the statute that relates to them, where they can discover the state's residency requirements:

1. A person who has physically resided in Montana as the person's principal or primary home or place of abode for 180 consecutive days immediately before making application for any license is eligible to receive hunting, fishing, or trapping licenses.
2. A person who obtains residency may continue to be a resident by physically residing in Montana as the person's principal or primary home or place of abode for not less that 120 days a year and by meeting the criteria above prior to making application for any resident hunting, fishing, or trapping license.
3. In addition to the above, a person shall meet the following criteria to be considered a resident:

a. the person's principal or primary home or place of abode is in Montana;
b. the person files Montana state income tax returns as a resident if required to file;
c. the person licenses and titles in Montana as required by law any vehicles that the person owns and operates in Montana;
d. the person does not possess or apply for any resident hunting, fishing, or trapping licenses from another state or country or exercise resident hunting, fishing, or trapping privileges in another state or country; and
e. if the person registers to vote, the person registers only in Montana.

Note that the statute, unlike the two application forms described above, says, "180 consecutive days immediately before making application" for the license, and it lists five behavioral requirements to depict what is meant by "resident," although the word, "legal," is not mentioned as it was on the Conservation form. In addition, number 2 above apparently refers to hunters who have acquired a hunting license in the past and now want to renew it. However, it does not indicate specifically which 120 days a year are required or whether they need to be consecutive. Number 3 above provides five questions, answerable with yes or no, that constitute a behavioral test of eligibility.

The final section of the statute, not relevant to our analysis, deals with students enrolled in a postsecondary educational institution out of state and Job Corps enrollees in Montana.

Turpin's lawyer was initially tempted to address the ambiguity of the statute at trial, but she eventually concluded that this effort would be unlikely to succeed even though the words "resident" and "residence" might offer a possible avenue of attack. One reason to question the statute is that most dictionary definitions of "residence" define it as the act of living or regularly staying at or in some place for some time for the discharge of duty or the enjoyment of a benefit. This could be the average hunter's understanding of this word, but *Black's Law Dictionary* defines "residence" differently (emphasis added):

> Personal presence at some place of abode with no present intention of definite and early removal with purpose to remain for an undetermined period, not infrequently, but *not necessarily combined with design to stay permanently*... residence is something more than mere physical presence and something less than domicile... the terms "resident" and "residence" have *no precise legal meaning*... a person may have only one legal domicile at one time, but he *may have more than one residence.*

While *Black's Law Dictionary* says "residence'" and "domicile" are not the same things, Montana statutes use the terms variably. For example, the general instructions to the Montana code (MCA 1–1–215) say: "Where statutes refer only to 'residence' and not 'domicile,' the courts have generally held that the word, 'residence' will be construed to mean practically the same thing as 'domicile.'" The expressions, "generally held" and "practically the same thing," offered a ray of hope, because these expressions are far from conclusive. Nor are Montana's statutes consistent in their use of the words. The state's Department of Revenue code (MCA 15–30–101) uses "domicile" consistently throughout. The code relating to motor vehicle registration (MCA 61–3–712) differentiates these words, saying: "the word 'residence' may not be confused with the word, 'domicile.'" Other Montana statutes vary, including the state's Election Provisions code (MCA 13–1–112), which uses "residence" 13 times, "habitation" once, and "home" once, but never mentions "domicile" at all.

After considerable discussion, we decided that there were at least two reasons why it seemed futile to argue over the potential ambiguity of "domicile." One is that few people have actually ever heard of the word, "domicile." On the other hand, ordinary people know and recognize "residence," and it would be difficult to base a defense on a word that is commonly understood. Legal language generally has problems in translating legal concepts into lay terms and concepts so in this case, the statute may have used "residence" out of concern for the layperson's ability to grasp the legal concept clearly. The second reason is that the prospective hunter could simply lie about his principle residence and then the government would have the difficult task of proving that the answer was a lie. Answers to the five-question behavioral test for determining eligibility are probably easier for the government to use.

In the end, Turpin's lawyer decided that even though the statute seemed a bit murky, attacking it could prove difficult. A review of Montana case law precedents revealed such statements as, "Where statutes refer only to residence and not to domicile, the courts have generally held that the word 'residence' will be constructed to mean practically the same as 'domicile'" (*Duckworth v. District Court*, 107 M 97, 80 P2d 367 (1938)). It's possible that one could also construct an argument over the meaning of "practically the same" here, but the chance of winning would still be slim. Instead, she decided that a better defense would be to address the confusion that hunting license applicants have in understanding the ambiguity and vagueness of the Conservation and Application forms that they had to complete before they could get a hunting license.

STRATEGY 4: ATTACK THE METHOD OF DETERMINING INTENTIONS

Since the statute didn't appear to be vulnerable, we next turned our attention to the fact that the Montana code for hunting licenses seems to require the state to discover the intentions of the applicants. We noted that Montana codes for other state statutory requirements, such as Election Provisions and Motor Vehicles, face the issue of intent head on, stating: "This residence need not be coupled with the *intent* to live or conduct the business there on a permanent basis" (MCA 61–3–712). Election rules use the words, "intend" or "intention" in each provision, such as "the individual has the *intention* of returning" (MCA 13–1–112).

Looking outside the state's statutes, we found that "intent" is also used in the state of Washington's statute relating to public education (28B.15.012 4), which defines the resident or non-resident status of students as follows (emphasis added):

> The permanent domicile shall denote a person's true, fixed and permanent home and place of habitation. It is the place where the student *intends* to remain, and to which the student expects to return when the student leaves without *intending* to establish a new domicile elsewhere.

In contrast, the Montana Application for a hunting license omits any overt mention of an applicant's intentions. Instead, it uses the five-question requirement noted above as a behavioral test in which it tries to discover such intentions by inference:

1. residing in Montana as principle abode for 180 consecutive days;
2. filing Montana income tax if required to file;
3. licensing motor vehicles owned or used in Montana;
4. having hunting licenses in no other states or countries; and
5. registering to vote only in Montana.

Hypothetically, persons who own homes in several places, who maintain vehicles licensed in Montana, who are already wealthy enough to require no new income on which to file tax reports, who haven't applied for hunting licenses elsewhere, and who don't vote at all could satisfy four of these five behavioral tests. This hypothetical example was consistent with Turpin's case. His only problem was behavioral test question number 1 above, the requirement about applicants having in more than one "principle abode." It could be argued that if the hunting license statute wanted to distinguish between multiple residences and only one legally sanctioned residence, the behavioral test simply could have asked which of the applicants' residences they *intend* as their single primary domicile or residence. In this way, the question of reported intentions would be clearly designated. If factual evidence could be established that applicants lied about this, a case for false statements would then have to be made.

It would seem that when answers relating to a person's intent are critical in determining issues of legality that can be litigated, the person's signed statement of intent might trump any behavioral state guidelines used to determine, even by inference, a person's innocence or guilt at trial. But in the Montana hunting license code, unlike its state codes for motor vehicles and elections, applicants are not directly asked about their intentions. Instead, the requirements try to determine the applicants' intentions from their answers to the five-question behavioral test.

So the question for the defense lawyer here was whether to pursue the appropriateness of inferring intentions through this set of five criteria or determining the applicants' intentions directly by asking simply "do you intend to be considered a legal resident?" After informal consultation with various law professors who discouraged this defense strategy, she decided against it. Montana chooses to grant hunting benefits to a class of people defined by the five behavioral questions in the statute and represented on the Application form. No doubt the state believes that its definition is easier to administer. And it probably is, because the five questions may be considered more objective than a question about intent would be. Intent is a difficult thing to prove, especially when answers can be outright falsehoods. Having abandoned this approach, there was then only one avenue left for the defense: to conduct a survey the opinions, feelings, and beliefs about the Application form with a representative population of users.

STRATEGY 5: CONDUCTING A USER SURVEY

Although there was much that could be said about the linguistic ambiguity and vagueness of the Conservation and Application forms and possibly even the statute, the defense lawyer then decided that presenting the rural jury with what might seem complex linguistic arguments about ambiguity might not be as effective as presenting results of a survey that would reveal the way average Montanans actually understand what is required of them on their hunting license applications. I do not do survey work of that type, so another expert was brought in for the purpose of determining whether the Conservation and Application forms were understandable.

The survey questions focused on the same vagueness and ambiguity discussed earlier as strategies 1 and 2, including the lack of necessary information that was in the statute but not available on the Application form, the infelicitous design and sequence of the Application form, the confusing statements about both the 180- and 120-day residence requirements, and the vague meanings of "immediately prior to" and "all statements on this form are true and correct." My earlier linguistic analysis framed most of the questions on the survey. The results of the survey strongly favored the defense, and this strategy apparently worked well, for Turpin was acquitted on his felony perjury charge.

After considerable discussion, the defense lawyer determined (wisely I believe) that her most efficient avenue of defense was not in the apparently arbitrary or ambiguous use of "resident" in the Application form and statute, not in the five-question behavioral test to determine who could reap the benefits of a hunting license, and not whether the state inferred legality without asking for it directly. The major problems lay in the Conservation and Application forms themselves, which desperately needed to be redesigned and reworded. The jury readily agreed with this approach, probably because it was so easy to understand.

The intelligence gatherers and law enforcement officers did the best they could. It was up to the intelligence analyst, in this case the prosecutor, to decide what to do with the evidence that her investigators had collected. Hunting is a very important thing to Montanans, so the prosecutor apparently believed that violating hunting laws would incense jurors against wealthy "outsiders" like Turpin. She was wrong. Her strategy backfired because the jury was incensed instead by the inadequacies of the confusing forms that *all* Montana hunters have to fill out. The defense attorney came to understand this and decided on a strategy in which the jury found the inadequacies of the bureaucracy to be greater than any possible predisposition to disfavor wealthy newcomers being allowed to hunt in their state. After all, this could happen to them too.

SECTION III

Perjury and the ill-fated shipping vessel, *Khian Sea*

This section is unlike the others because it is a very complex case dealing with two separate perjury trials relating to exactly the same disputed events. It's necessary for the experts who assist lawyers in such cases to know the basic backgrounds of the cases they analyze, especially when the relevant fields of knowledge are so different from their own. In the following two chapters it's important for readers to know some of the basics of the commercial overseas shipping industry in order to understand the accusations and the defendants' testimony. Since these two cases grow out of the same industry procedures and alleged perjurious acts, it seemed useful to provide the necessary background information only once, which I do here.

A large shipping vessel called the *Khian Sea* left the port of Philadelphia in April 1986 bound for Freeport, the Bahamas, loaded with 15,000 tons of incinerator ash. It sailed around the world trying to unload the ash, and after seven years, the courts were still trying to learn what happened to the cargo that disappeared somewhere between Philadelphia, where it started its voyage, and Singapore, where it arrived empty in 1988. The complicated story culminated in the indictments of two shipping executives who, as it turned out, had little or nothing to say that could explain where the ash went or who was responsible. The following rather specialized information about the shipping business will be helpful to readers as they follow the perjury indictments of these two executives.

The major players here were the owner of the ship, Lilly Shipping Company, the company that chartered the vessel, Amalgamated Shipping Company, and the company that served as the shipping agent for the charterer, Coastal Shipping.

As the chartering company, Amalgamated more or less rented the ship for a specific time period, using what is called a time charter, an agreement similar to a lease. The shipping agent, Coastal, was hired by the chartering company to make arrangements for pilots and berths, to coordinate with local authorities, to hire stevedores, to supervise the loading and unloading, and to commission tugboats to guide the *Khian Sea* in and out of ports in the United States. Coastal's job also included arranging for local shipping agents to do the same things in foreign ports wherever the ship docked.

Normally, the time charter reflects estimates about the amount of time needed for a ship to load, sail, arrive at its destination port, and discharge its cargo. A time lease contract is written to cover this estimated period. The *Khian Sea,* however, ran into severe difficulties and its time charter expired before it managed to dock at its designated port. It was well within the limits of the time charter for the ship to sail from Philadelphia and unload its cargo in the Bahamas, but things did not go as planned, leading up to the eventual perjury indictments of William Dowd and William Reilly.

The series of events in this case can become a bit confusing, partly because of the names and positions held by the people involved. Therefore, readers will benefit from a scorecard. During the time when the *Khian Sea* events took place, defendant William Reilly was vice-president of Amalgamated, the company that chartered the vessel from Lilly, the owner of the ship. At that same time, John Dowd (defendant William Dowd's father) was the president of Coastal

Shipping, the company that served as the shipping agent for this voyage. John Dowd's son, defendant William Dowd, was vice-president of Coastal at the time of this fated voyage, but after Reilly resigned as vice-president of Amalgamated, William Dowd left Coastal and became president of Amalgamated.

While he was still vice-president of Amalgamated, William Reilly made arrangements with the governor of the Bahamas to offload 15,000 tons of incinerator ash there. Coastal Shipping's John Dowd signed on as the shipping agent, although his son, William Dowd, was the person most involved. The Bahamas had planned to use the ash as landfill for a new low-income housing project. But while the ship was still on its way to the Bahamas, media articles informed the governor that the ash was toxic and hazardous. Because of the furor over this, the governor changed his mind just as the ship was about to dock and refused to give the *Khian Sea* permission to enter the port.

Reilly quickly began to negotiate with ports in other Caribbean countries while, at the same time, he hired soil experts and agronomists to test the ash and report their findings to government entities so that he might be able to convince other countries to accept the cargo. One such country was Costa Rica, which also was planning to build low-income housing in low-lying areas where they planned new housing projects. But by the time the *Khian Sea* neared the port, Costa Rican officials also were told that the ash was toxic, leading them to cancel their agreement to accept it. In spite of the testing that had now satisfied the U.S. Environmental Protection Agency (EPA) that the ash was not toxic and dangerous, the negative media frenzy was repeated. Reilly explained to Costa Rican officials that this same ash had been found acceptable in Washington, D.C., where a million and a half tons of it had been used as landfill under St. Elizabeth's Hospital, as well as in other cities, including Tampa, Florida, and in other U.S. building sites that required landfill. This did not change the minds of the Costa Ricans.

The *Khian Sea* then sailed from Costa Rica to Honduras, experiencing the same rejection, and from there to Panama, where General Noreiga was still in control. By that time the EPA had repudiated its earlier report that the ash was nontoxic, and while the ship was waiting in harbor, several of Noreiga's soldiers boarded the ship, captured some of the crew, and hauled them off to jail on specious charges for a brief period, after which the ship continued its journey.

Haiti was the *Khian Sea*'s next stop, where Reilly had also received an agreement from the proper local officials to unload the ash. Things went well at first, but after the ship had offloaded 4,000 tons, Haiti experienced a government upheaval that halted the unloading operation. Meanwhile, the government heeded the same adverse publicity generated by media in the United States and elsewhere. Threats to the seamen became so intense that Amalgamated ordered the captain to stop unloading and return to Philadelphia immediately.

The *Khian Sea* reached Philadelphia in March 1988, after eighteen months in the Caribbean area. Coastal, the shipping agent, had paid all the expenses, wages of the captain and crew, fuel costs, and port charges. Coastal billed Amalgamated for these costs, but by that time Amalgamated was bankrupt and could not reimburse Coastal. The plan then was to unload the remaining 11,000 tons of ash in Philadelphia, where this all began, but unknown persons set the pier afire before this could happen. A United States Coast Guard officer who was in charge of the pier told Reilly that Greenpeace, the organization thought to have originated the news accounts that the ash was toxic, had told him that the ash would never unload in Philadelphia. Reilly then contacted a dozen other Eastern and Southern states but received the same negative responses.

In May 1988, the Khian Sea, still loaded with the ash, left the Philadelphia harbor covertly in the middle of the night. Reilly was shocked because the captain sailed without the required permission of the Coast Guard. Once he knew the ship had left port, Reilly called Amalgamated to inform Dowd about what had happened. Dowd advised Reilly to notify the Coast Guard that the captain had been suffering from mental and emotional distress because of the constant harassment and allegedly inaccurate news stories saying that the ash was toxic. The *Khian Sea*'s crew had not set foot on dry land for two years and were fearful about what else might happen to them as a result of those stories. Because the ship left port without authority, the courts could have brought criminal or civil charges against Amalgamated, but possibly recognizing the extremity of this situation, the company received only a token $1000 fine for this procedural infraction.

When the *Khian Sea* left the Philadelphia port, its destination was now unknown to everyone, including the captain, who finally cabled Reilly and asked, "What do we do now?" Reilly reported that his answer was, "I don't know." Reilly and Dowd then devised a plan in which Reilly would fly to Dakar, Senegal, to try to make arrangements to have the ash unloaded there. When the officials there also said "no" to this plan, the Khian Sea sailed on, this time through the Strait of Gibraltar and on to Yugoslavia, where it was allowed to dock, but only for needed repairs.

While on this journey, Lilly Shipping Company sold the vessel to new owners, and the official transfer of ownership took place when the ship docked in Yugoslavia. Reilly went there next, because when ships change ownership, the charterer is responsible for arranging necessary repairs. In any case, after three years the time charter had now expired, but the requirements of time charters meant that Amalgamated was also responsible for reporting the condition of the ship when it docked at port.

After the repairs were finished and with the cargo of ash still in its hold, the *Khian Sea*, under new ownership and with a new name and a new captain, sailed from Yugoslavia and finally docked in Singapore with no incinerator ash on board. The U.S. government naturally wondered what had happened to the ash. Obviously, it was offloaded somewhere, quite likely in either the Indian or Pacific Oceans, but since it was illegal to dump the ash in the ocean, the United States government was concerned enough about this to subpoena both William Reilly and William Dowd, who was originally with Coastal but later became president of Amalgamated. By now both companies had filed for bankruptcy.

The following two chapters report the use of linguistic analysis in the separate perjury cases of Reilly and Dowd. The depositions and trials were at separate times and the defendants used different law firms to defend them. The lawyers for both defendants retained me for whatever assistance I could offer.

(7)
Perjury charges for a shipping company executive

In early January 1990, the federal grand jury in Wilmington, Delaware, conducted an investigation to determine whether the *Khian Sea* had violated Title 33 US Code, Section 1411, which prohibits transportation of any material from the United States for the purpose of dumping it into the ocean. The prosecutor wanted to learn whether any persons had knowledge about where the incinerator ash on the *Khian Sea* was offloaded. He determined that such persons included William Dowd, president of Coastal Carriers and the agent for the owners and operators of the *Khian Sea*, who was then called to testify about this matter in February 1990.

Dowd was subsequently indicted for making false statements, based largely on his following answers during his testimony before the grand jury:

Juror: Do you know what happened to the ash?
Dowd: No.
Juror: You have no idea?
Dowd: No, I don't. I honestly have not been on that ship for two and a half years.
Juror: Seeing how you had all this concern of not being able to unload this ash, you didn't ask anybody where it went?
Dowd: Who is there to ask?

Juror: I guess you could start with asking the captain. He ought to know where it went.

Dowd: They say he's a funny guy. The first time I met him, Honduran person, he said "The ash is gone." And I said—

Juror: Just said "gone", but you didn't want to know where it went?

Dowd: No, I didn't ask and I don't know. All right? Nor did he tell me.

Subsequently, based largely on his testimony, Dowd was tried for perjury in June 1993. His lawyer retained me to analyze the evidence in the case. The three major issues that the jury had to consider involved Dowd's answers to these questions in his grand jury testimony:

1. What happened to the ash?
2. Seeing how you had all of this concern of not being able to unload this ash, you didn't ask anybody where it went?
3. You had "no idea" where it went?

THE LITERAL TRUTH VERSUS FIGURATIVE LANGUAGE

Despite arguments and linguistic evidence presented by Dowd's defense, it was apparent that the jury believed Dowd did not tell the truth when he indicated that he had "no idea" what had happened to the incinerator ash. We can't know what was going on in the jurors' thinking process, of course, but they convicted him for committing perjury.

There is always the possibility that the jurors were justifiably bothered by the fact that because *someone* was responsible for dumping the incinerator ash in the ocean, they felt it necessary to place the blame on a specific person. It's more likely, however, that the jurors didn't understand the difference between literal truth and figurative speech. Did Dowd mean that he could not conjure up any idea about what happened to the ash? This would seem pretty silly, since it had to have been dumped somewhere. Or did he simply use a common figurative expression indicating that he didn't really know for sure? Or was he being deceptive here because he really knew who dumped the ash and where it was dumped? If the latter, the jury even could have believed that Dowd actually gave the captain the specific instruction to dump the ash in the ocean.

As noted in chapter 1, the literal truth issue in Dowd's case bears some similarity to the case of *Bronston v. United States,* when at trial the jury thought it was likely that Bronston knowingly and intentionally interpreted the word, "you," in the question, "Do you have any bank accounts in Swiss banks?" to refer to his company rather than to himself:

Q: Do you have any bank accounts in Swiss banks, Mr. Bronston?
A: No, sir.
Q: Have you ever?
A: The company had an account there for about six months, in Zurich.

Bronston indeed once had held a personal bank account in a Geneva bank for some five years before his trial, but he did not hold such an account at the time he was questioned in court. His answer above avoided the second question, "Have you ever" by giving a literally truthful answer (to a question that arguably wasn't asked) concerning his company's assets. Subsequently, the jury found Bronston guilty of perjury. But the matter didn't end there.

Bronston appealed this verdict, noting that the key question was imprecise and claiming that there were multiple interpretations, further adding that although Bronston's testimony was not responsive, it was concededly truthful. But the Court of Appeals upheld the District Court decision and ruled:

> An answer containing half of the truth which also constitutes a lie by negative implication, when the answer is intentionally given in place of the responsive answer called for by a proper question, is perjury.

Bronston then took the case to the U.S. Supreme Court, which ruled in favor of Bronston and concluded:

> The problem of the ambiguity of the question is not free from doubt, but we need not reach that issue . . . Even assuming, as we do, that the question asked petitioner specifically focused on petitioner's personal bank accounts, we conclude that the federal perjury statute cannot be construed to sustain a conviction based on petitioner's answer.

The Court then made a distinction between casual conversation and the type of language used in the courtroom:

> There is indeed an implication in the answer to the second question that there was never a personal bank account; in casual conversation this interpretation might reasonably be drawn. But we are not dealing with casual conversation and the statute does not make it a criminal act for a witness to willfully state any material matter that implies any material matter that he does not believe to be truth.

Finally, the Supreme Court placed the problem on the prosecutor:

> It is the responsibility of the lawyer to probe, and testimonial interrogation and cross-examination in particular, is a probing,

> pressing form of inquiry. If a witness evades, it is the lawyer's responsibility to recognize the evasion and bring the witness back to the mark, to flush out the whole truth with the tools of adversary examination.... The perjury statute is not to be loosely construed, nor the statute invoked simply because a wily witness succeeds in derailing the questioner—so long as the witness speaks the *literal truth.*

From the Bronston decision, we learn that courtroom testimony can be literally true even if it is not responsive, that courtroom language has a higher standard than everyday conversation, and that if there is ambiguity in a witness's answer, it is up to the prosecutor to request clarification that will lead to clarity of response.

Dowd's language took a slightly different path. He was responding to a grand juror's common figurative expression, "*You have no idea* what happened to the ash?" Dowd's defense argued that his answer of "no" to this question was equivalent to saying, "I don't know." At the time of this writing, a search on Google showed hundreds of citations of "I don't know," none of which suggest any other meaning than simply not knowing the answer to a question. It's how we talk. Dowd's answer was that he had no idea, didn't know, and was not willing to guess what happened to the ash.

THE GRAND JURY SPEECH EVENT AND CONVERSATIONAL MAXIMS

So why did the trial jury believe Dowd's answer was not truthful? To try to answer this question, I examined Dowd's entire grand jury testimony to see if there were any clues that might lead the jury to this conclusion. The *Bronston* court ruled that courtroom language was different from everyday conversation. A good discourse analysis strategy is to begin by examining the courtroom speech event itself. This setting brings with it certain presuppositions about what is and what is not appropriate. As noted throughout this book, hearings and trials are fact-finding settings in which witnesses are expected to observe Grice's maxims of cooperation:

1. Be as informative as is required; no less so or more so.
2. Say what you know to be true and do not say that for which you lack evidence.
3. Be relevant.
4. Avoid obscurity of expressions and be brief and orderly.

The setting of the grand jury speech event is obviously not conducive to speculation or irrelevant guesses about what a witness reports (maxims 1, 2, and 3). The question/answer format also dictates that the witnesses' time to talk is controlled by the questioner and that their answers must focus on only that which is asked (maxims 1 and 4). This setting is also is also conducive to avoiding restatements of already known or reported information (maxim 3).

By the time the critical questions were asked, Dowd had already testified that it was his understanding that the ship had no ash on it when it arrived in Singapore:

Grand juror:	When you were in Singapore . . . was the ship still loaded with ash?
Dowd:	No.
Grand Juror:	Do you know what happened to the ash?
Dowd:	No.

It is clear that Dowd had already said that he was fully aware that the ship was empty at that time and that he did not know what had happened to the ash.

A possible issue here could have arisen from Dowd's answer to the questioner who asked what happened to the ash. For him, the maxim of relevance obtained (maxim 3). There was no need to repeat what he had already reported. But suppose his answer had been, "It was dumped somewhere between Yugoslavia and Singapore." Besides the risk of violating the maxim of relevance, there were two other reasons why he couldn't say this. First, he had no personal or verifiable knowledge that this had actually happened. Second, it would have sounded inappropriately flippant to say something as obvious as this (maxim of relevance again). Instead, Dowd interpreted the question, "what happened to," as a request about whether he actually knew where, how, or when the ash was removed. This interpretation was perfectly possible, as evidenced by the grand jury's unwillingness to indict him of perjury for not knowing what happened to it. They focused instead on his statement that he had "no idea" what had happened to the ash. In short, they indicted him for not being willing to speculate. Now we need to discover why he was unwilling to infer, make guesses, or speculate.

Context is the obvious place to look. Throughout his testimony, Dowd had been careful to state only that for which he had evidence (maxim 2). He followed the expectations one has for this particular speech event and setting, testifying only about what he personally experienced or found to be true, based on respectable, authoritative documentation. Adhering to the cooperative principle yields the assumption that the questions are orderly and transparent (maxim 4), especially when the questioner holds the power in the interaction. Dowd's response that he had "no idea" must be assumed to be relevant (maxim 3) to the series of questions he was asked and, therefore, it was an orderly outgrowth of the preceding questions and answers. His answer was contextually dependent on, and conveyed the same meaning as, his previous answers of "no." His earlier answer that the ship arrived in Singapore with no ash aboard clarified that he did not interpret the grand juror's later question to be asking him whether or not the cargo had been offloaded somewhere. Of course it had. Everyone knew that. Common sense.

In the context of this speech event, the questioner's word, "idea," is not to be associated with the literal meaning found in dictionaries, a thought or concept. When people say, "I have no idea," they are simply saying that they do not know for sure and at the present time are unwilling to guess or speculate. Its use is figurative and formulaic, much like saying "I can't imagine why," or "it beats me," or "God only knows."

Meanings conveyed by formulaic, figurative expressions are determined by their context, not by the literal meanings of their individual words. In a formulaic expression like "I have no idea," one can't parse the literal meanings of the individual words to construct its meaning. The meaning is found in the context of the entire unit itself, acknowledged by current understanding of the expression's common use in society.

In any case, it was the questioner, not Dowd, who had introduced the formulaic expression, "you have no idea." Dowd merely responded "no" to the question. The question conveyed the meaning of "you're not sure?" Not surprisingly, Dowd's response treated this question as a request for a confirmation of the certainty of Dowd's previous answer to the question, "what happened to the ash."

Based on this grand jury testimony, however, the prosecutor concluded that he now had enough to indict Dowd for perjury—indicative of dangerously weak intelligence analysis.

DOWD'S TRIAL TESTIMONY

At his subsequent trial, Dowd's responses contained many of the same responses to the similarly worded questions that he was asked when he appeared before the grand jury:

Prosecutor:	Do you have any knowledge as you sit here today, Mr. Dowd, as to what happened to the incinerator residue that was on board the vessel when it departed Yugoslavia?
Dowd:	No, sir.
Prosecutor:	Do you know of any means by which you might find out what happened to the incinerator residue that was on board the vessel?
Dowd:	No, sir.
...	
Prosecutor:	Mr. Dowd, what notice, what information have you received concerning disposal of the ash aboard the ship that was called the *Khian Sea*? What written notice have you gotten regarding the disposal of the ash aboard the *Khian Sea*?
Dowd:	The only notice we received about disposal of the cargo was a notice from Romo Shipping [the new owner], their vice-president, saying that the cargo was disposed of... Last week I received a copy that was signed by the American Bureau of Shipping that the vessel had no cargo on board when they inspected the vessel in Singapore.
...	
Prosecutor:	Mr. Dowd, I'm unclear. Do you have any actual first-hand knowledge whether or not the ash was removed from the *Khian Sea*?
Dowd:	No. Just the two reports I received in writing.

To 97 of the 106 questions he was asked at trial, Dowd's answers were based on what he knew first-hand or from reliable sources. He did manage to speculate nine times, but these were not about anything relevant or material to his charges. His first eight speculative answers were:

- I understand the ship was sold to an international company.
- I think Coastal is a bidder. I believe the ship was in North Africa.
- Reilly was gone two or three weeks probably.
- Reilly was generally back in America.
- I assume he was notified.
- I would think Reilly was back in America.
- I don't think Coastal did any business with Romo.
- I presume Amalgamated was paying their usual fees.

Dowd's reluctance to speculate about material issues dominated throughout his testimony. He carefully distinguished what he knew and could verify but he wouldn't venture a guess about anything for which he was not certain. He did this, despite the fact that the judge did not prevent him from expressing his belief about what might have happened, as his ninth speculative answer shows (emphasis added):

Prosecutor:	Do you have any understanding one way or the other as to whether or not Romo Shipping Corp. agreed to purchase the incinerator residue?
Dowd:	I had to draw a conclusion which I don't know what their thinking was. They did accept the vessel. The vessel did have ash on. So I think it's logical to conclude that they knew it had ash on it.
Prosecutor:	Where did the vessel go when it departed Yugoslavia?
Dowd:	From the press reports I've seen, it went to Singapore.
Prosecutor:	I'm going to object, your honor, *unless he has actual knowledge.*
The Court:	Well, he's one of the parties to this suit, and I think it may be material certainly on a contempt hearing

as to what his beliefs may have been. So I'll overrule the objection.

Dowd: Whether it stopped at ports en route, I have no knowledge.

Prosecutor: So the only knowledge that you have as to the movement of the vessel comes from what you've read in the newspapers. Is that correct?

Dowd: Yes, sir.

It's curious here that the prosecutor objected when Dowd admittedly speculated after he was urged to do so by the judge, while at the same time Dowd was charged with perjury because he refused to speculate about what happened to the ash. In the above exchange, Dowd's speculation was based on logic. Romo Shipping owned the ship loaded with ash when it left Yugoslavia and it still owned it when it arrived empty in Singapore. This logic was not that of a genius, but logic made him willing to speculate about this material aspect of the case. But he remained firm in his unwillingness to speculate about who, when, where, and how it was dumped. That was a level of guessing that he was simply unwilling to reach. He consistently repeated that he didn't know "what happened" to the ash and that he had no means to find this out. He further testified that what he did know was based on two reliable written notices but that he had no first-hand knowledge about how the ash disappeared, where this may have occurred, and who was responsible for the dumping. Dowd's trial testimony was completely consistent with what he said before the grand jury.

It is often useful in criminal cases to compare the indictment with the facts that were brought out at trial. One such charge in the indictment was that Dowd claimed to not know that the ash was unloaded. Neither his grand jury nor his trial testimony supported this charge. Dowd testified that he received notice that the ash had been disposed of when he subsequently filed for bankruptcy. A second charge in the indictment was that Dowd knew that the ash was dumped in the Indian Ocean. Oddly enough, the prosecutor never even asked Dowd about this at trial.

CLARIFICATION OF AMBIGUITY

One of the points made in the U.S. Supreme Court's ruling in the *Bronston* case was that it is the *prosecutor's* responsibility to clarify ambiguities with follow-up questions. In Dowd's trial, the prosecutor did not request clarification of potentially ambiguous language. Instead, it was the defendant, Dowd, who tried to request clarification about certain of the prosecutor's ambiguous questions. This happened many times and the following are only illustrative:

> Prosecutor: How is it that you're employed?
> Dowd: During what time?
>
> • • •
>
> Prosecutor: Well, you could negotiate on behalf of your client, couldn't you?
> Dowd: Negotiate about what? Ask me specific questions. I'm glad to help.
>
> • • •
>
> Prosecutor: Does he have a title or work for a company that you know?
> Dowd: Which time frame?

The prosecutor was particularly careless in his use of pronouns. Dowd frequently asked him to clarify with questions like, "Does the 'you' mean me or who is 'you?'" To a different question it fell to Dowd to observe, "It's very important to know what the 'we' and the 'they' and 'you' here mean in what you're talking about." The obligation to identify possible ambiguity was apparently foreign to this prosecutor.

As bad as the intelligence analysis was in this case, a more serious problem was the lack of fair and effective questioning by the prosecutor. The trial jury entered an acquittal about "what happened to the ash" and "why he didn't ask anybody where it went" but found him guilty for saying he had no idea where it went. After the trial, Dowd's lawyer told me sadly, "It's an understatement to say that this resolution was a surprise to everyone, including the prosecution."

(8)

Perjury charges for another shipping company executive

The second trial in the *Khian Sea* case related to the perjury indictment of William Reilly, which took place at a different time and with a different jury, prosecutor, judge, and defense lawyer. He was called twice before the grand jury to testify under oath about his involvement in the *Khian Sea* adventures. His first appearance was in January 1990 and his second about a month later. As a result of his testimony, Reilly was indicted in January 1993 on one count of perjury. Only one brief portion of his February testimony was cited in his indictment (emphasis added):

> Q: Do you have any knowledge as of today, Mr. Reilly, as to *what happened* to the incinerator ash on board the vessel?
>
> A: No, sir.
>
> Q: Do you have any knowledge as to *the means by which it might be ascertained what happened* to the residue on board the vessel?
>
> A: No, sir.

Immediately following this passage, the indictment continued (emphasis added):

> The aforesaid statements and answers of the defendant, William P. Reilly, that *he had no knowledge of what happen* [*sic*] to the

> incinerator ash residue on board the *Khian Sea* were false in that the defendant, William P. Reilly, then and there *well knew* that the incinerator ash residue onboard the *Khian Sea* had been discharged, *disposed of* and off-loaded from the *Khian Sea* by dumping the incinerator ash residue into the water in and around the Atlantic Ocean and Indian Ocean. All in violation of Title 18, United States Code, Section 1623(a).

Shortly after he was indicted, Reilly's attorney retained me for linguistic assistance in this case. A few days after I agreed to work on this case, an attorney for the Environmental Crimes Section of the Department of Justice called me about consulting with him as a linguistics expert. As he began to describe his case, I had to stop him and explain that I had been retained previously by the defense attorney in that same case. I point out this incident here because if and when the prosecution attempts to prevent an expert witness from testifying at trial, it's always helpful to be able to respond that the prosecutors themselves wanted the expert to perform that very analysis. This was such a case. Prosecutors often object to expert witnesses for the defense, claiming that the experts work only for that side and therefore can be considered as biased hired guns. In my experience, prosecutors seldom call on linguists to be expert witnesses. They have called me only a few times, most of which were to prevent me from testifying for the other side, a fact that I learned subsequently from two defense attorneys who had formerly been prosecutors who had called on my services on behalf of the government, but then failed to use my services.

Reilly's second appearance before the grand jury contained 140 pages of transcript. Based only on the passage cited in the indictment, it's obvious that the government believed Reilly had lied about two things: (1) having no knowledge of what happened to the cargo of incinerator ash and (2) about how he (or anyone else) could ascertain knowledge of its disappearance. In short, the prosecutor said that Reilly falsely testified that he didn't know what happened and that he didn't even know how to find out what happened.

As noted in chapter 7, analysis of courtroom testimony begins with an understanding of the structure, rules, and expectations of this speech event. Following customary procedure, the prosecutor first issued a subpoena to Reilly, requiring him to provide certain facts such as records, agreements, memoranda, journals, ledgers, cancelled checks, and many other documents, which Reilly provided in a timely fashion. Now came the serious speech event in which the grand jury would examine and evaluate the facts in order to determine whether to indict Reilly. It was important for the grand jury to learn these facts because this information framed the direction and scope of the questioning. Indeed, this was Reilly's schema of the event.

SCHEMA

Human cognitive processes mediate the comprehension of and in an event. One such process is called schema. Research on schema began in the 1970s using story schemata (Rummelhart 1975) as a set of rules for segmenting, identifying, and manipulating story constituents (Van Dijk 1985, 94). Readers and listeners develop their understanding of a story through their past and present experiences with real-world events, which they then apply to the new events and words in a story. In short, they see and understand things from their own perspective and world knowledge, their schemas.

This same cognitive process applies to expository events, such as grand jury hearings. Witnesses in these events understand and interpret questions based on their past and present world knowledge. They utilize their own schemas when they respond to the questions, and then try to account for and verify appropriateness according to those schemas (Van Dijk 1985, 95). Just as "once upon a time" activates a listener's schema of a fairy tale, so the questions in a grand jury hearing activate the schema of testifying about only that which is factual and can be verified during that speech event. This would eliminate speculation and guesswork, which would seem, in the witness's schema, to be inappropriate. From Reilly's responses in this hearing, it is clear that his schema was based on his understanding of what a grand jury speech event required of him, as the following will show.

THE INDICTMENT

The ensuing indictment focused on Reilly's answers and concluded that Reilly lied about facts that he actually knew to be true. Focused as he was on the schema that he was to provide true and verifiable facts in this hearing, Reilly was surprised when only a few minutes into his examination the prosecutor asked him to speculate (emphasis added):

Q: You *don't have to be exactly familiar* to talk to us. I want to know who you *sort of think might* be stockholders in Copaco...

A: That would be Michael Dowd. I think that's about the only one that I can with some assurance indicate...

Q: ...I want to take you one step further removed. Who else *do you think might* be in that?

A: Counsel, I'm speculating and I think you're looking for *facts.*

Q: We are looking for facts, but *we're going to take a little speculation* about this particular question...

A: Counsel, I respectfully request that I not be forced to speculate in these very important matters.

After this exchange, Reilly's effort to avoid speculation continued, while the prosecutor continued to try to elicit his assumptions, inferences, and guesses. This made Reilly very careful to identify clearly and explicitly whether he was speculating or reporting facts. From that point on, when he succumbed to questions requiring him to speculate, Reilly carefully marked his answers with qualifiers such as, "I believe," "I think," "I am not certain," and "I'll have to check my records." When he had no memory at all, he said "I don't remember" and when he didn't know, he said, "I don't know." Throughout, he was very careful to make a clear distinction between his primary sources of known facts and his secondary sources of information, as the following examples illustrate:

1. Direct, experiential, personal knowledge:
   "my direct knowledge is that the stockholders..."
2. Knowledge that he could officially document:
   "I had seen a report from the American Bureau..."
   "I had seen court records..."
3. Awareness of something:
   "I was aware of the negotiations but I wasn't involved in them"
   "I was aware by the newspaper coverage..."
4. Knowledge that he got from other specified people:
   "I was advised by a representative of Lilly..."
   "Mr. Dowd advised me..."
   "That is what I was told. I had no verification of that."
   "It was conveyed to me by the Coast Guard."
5. Unverified speculation, inference, or tentative knowledge:
   "I believe he's a stockholder"
   "This was probably in early December"
   "presumably they were made by either Amalgamated or..."
   "It may have been in Bejela."

I made charts citing each response that Reilly made in all of these five categories for his defense lawyer to use at trial. This information became important because it was necessary for the jury to understand the difference between factual knowledge and speculation in both the prosecutor's questions and in Reilly's answers, especially when it came time for the jury to determine what both parties meant by "what happened to," "know," and "disposed of."

THE MEANING OF "KNOW"

When the prosecutor asked, "do you *know* what happened to the ash," Reilly's schema of the fact-finding structure of this speech event led him to understand that he should report only that which he had perceived directly, knew or experienced factually, or had learned from an authoritative source. Since none of these obtained, he answered that he did not know. His response is supported by common understandings of what "know" means.

The *American Heritage Dictionary* defines the verb "know" as:

1. to perceive directly with the senses or mind . . . ;
2. to be certain of: regard as true beyond doubt;
3. to have practical understanding of or thorough experience with.

Reilly's answers to the prosecutor's questions followed his schema of the grand jury event and these common understandings of what "know" means. He provided facts that he perceived, was certain of, and had a practical understanding of through his personal experience. He carefully marked what he did not perceive directly, was not certain about, and did not personally experience.

THE MEANING OF "DISPOSED OF"

The same dictionary defines "dispose of" as follows:

1. to place, distribute or arrange in an orderly way;
2. to transfer to the control of another;
3. to get rid of something that is good to dispose of;
4. to deal with conclusively.

Reilly testified that did not *know* where or how the ash was disposed of and distributed, and whatever way this was done. He *knew,* along with everyone else, that it certainly was offloaded from the *Khian Sea* somewhere. Everyone *knew* this. He *knew* and testified that the vessel changed ownership in Yugoslavia while it still contained 11,000 tons of ash, so he *knew* that control had been transferred. Everyone also *knew* this. It's equally certain that disposing of the ash was thought to be a good thing because that was precisely what the ship had been trying to accomplish for over two years. Everyone *knew* this as well. He said that he had no knowledge, however, that could be considered conclusive or even useful to the court about how the ash was disposed of or who was responsible for this. Following his schema that the court wanted only factually based and verifiable evidence, Reilly indicated that he had no knowledge that could supplement anyone else's knowledge about that event.

THE MEANING OF "THE MEANS OF ASCERTAINING WHAT HAPPENED"

Finally, the indictment claimed Reilly was lying when he answered that he had no knowledge of "the means by which it might be ascertained what happened to the residue." This question appeared to be asking Reilly to relate any possibilities he could imagine about how, where, and by whom the ash was unloaded. By that point in his testimony, Reilly's reluctance to speculate, guess, or infer had been well established. He could have speculated that the new owner's captain had dumped the ash somewhere in the ocean, but maintaining his schema about the purpose of his testimony, he was unwilling to say this because he didn't know for sure. Besides, anyone could figure out that when a ship leaves a port loaded and is empty when it docks at another port, the cargo must have been offloaded at some point along its way. The oddity of this indictment is that almost anyone could offer essentially uninformed and unhelpful speculations. It was not clear why Reilly's unwillingness to do so could lead to his indictment for perjury.

It also remains unclear why the prosecutor maintained his own schema that Reilly actually knew more than this. Reilly testified clearly that he had only infrequent and brief radio contact with the ship after the captain decided to leave the Philadelphia port area without authorization and sailed out into the Atlantic Ocean. The captain did this without a known destination and without informing anyone of his plans, including Coastal Shipping and the U.S. Coast Guard. Reilly next learned from an authorized source that the ship had docked in Yugoslavia for repairs and was sold to new owners. Coastal was still responsible for assessing needed repairs, so Reilly went there to see that this was accomplished. By that time the previously negotiated time charter had expired, so Coastal's responsibility would end as soon as Reilly assessed the needed repairs. After that point, the ship was out of Coastal's authority as its shipping agent and there was no need for him to learn what happened thereafter.

REQUESTING CLARIFICATION

The Supreme Court's decision in *Bronston* can be recycled here. As noted earlier, the U.S. Supreme Court placed the burden on the questioner to clarify ambiguous answers by probing further and deeper to get the true facts.

Recall that throughout his testimony Reilly had been careful to specify whether his answers were: (1) from primary sources (direct, experiential, documented, or personal knowledge); (2) from secondary sources (awareness, from other people) or (3) assumptions and speculation.

The following imaginary exchange can show how the prosecutor might have followed up on the questions that led to Reilly's indictment:

Q: Do you have any knowledge as of today, Mr. Reilly, as to what happened to the incinerator ash on board the vessel?

A: No, sir.

Q: Let me be sure that I understand your answer. Are you basing this answer on your lack of direct and verifiable knowledge about this?

A: Yes, sir.

Q: Well then, are you willing to speculate about what happened to the ash?

A: Sir, I have no basis on which to speculate that would be different from anyone else's speculation.

Q: I see, well then do you have any direct, personal or experiential knowledge about the means by which someone could have dumped the residue on board the vessel?

A: No, sir. Like anyone else, I can only guess that it might have been the new captain who decided to dump the residue in the ocean somewhere.

One could argue, I suppose, that Reilly is the one who could have requested clarification about what the prosecutor meant by "what happened to" and "the means by which it might be ascertained." Since language exchanges are expected to be cooperative (Grice 1975), we might expect vagueness and ambiguity to be resolved by either or both of the parties. Even though the *Bronston* decision puts the burden on the prosecutor to clarify ambiguities, why didn't Reilly request clarification? There are at least three possible reasons.

First, the ongoing context of the exchange indicates that it's likely that he didn't realize that the question was ambiguous. He had already said repeatedly that he didn't know the fate of the ash, including when and where it was offloaded. And it was obvious to him that everyone realized that the only persons who could make that decision were the new owners of the ship, Romo Shipping, or the new captain of the vessel, who could decide to do this even though he didn't have the authority to do so without the ship owner's directive. Reilly's testimony was given before a grand jury, where he had no attorney present to object to the repetition of questions that previously had been asked and answered. Obviously, Reilly thought he already had answered this question several times and that his answer was clear and unambiguous.

The second likely reason Reilly didn't seek clarification was that he had some understanding of the requirements of a grand jury speech event and was committed to answering only that which he knew to be factual, from primary evidence of direct, experiential, personal knowledge. He had made clear that he did not have such knowledge from reliable, documented information that he received from reports or records. None of these could provide him with the requested answer. His only alternative would be to speculate, which, since he followed his schema to carefully testify only about known facts, he chose not to do.

The third reason why Reilly didn't request clarification is that he didn't recognize any ambiguity in his own answers and, in any case, he didn't have the power and control in this exchange. In order to clarify ambiguity, a listener first has to perceive that something is ambiguous. Apparently, Reilly thought that his "no" was unambiguous. Perhaps the prosecutor didn't recognize his own lack of clarity, but when superordinate questioners, including prosecutors, recognize ambiguity, no matter who creates it, it is their responsibility to manage the exchange in such a way that there is nothing ambiguous about their questions and no unresolved ambiguity in the responses of the subordinate speaker being questioned, as the U.S. Supreme Court said in its ruling in *Bronston*.

DECEPTION?

Since Reilly was ultimately convicted of perjury, the question of his possible deception should be considered. He didn't vary in what he said to the grand jury and at trial, so inconsistent or conflicting testimony can be ruled out. The prosecutor's intelligence gathering effort yielded no factual evidence that conflicted with what Reilly testified about. So rule that out also. Reilly did not give truthful but irrelevant answers to questions as Bronston did, so rule that out as well. If he hid truthful information from the prosecutor, this did not come out in their exchanges.

In short, there was no evidence of deception here. This prosecution was a good example of either inadequate intelligence gathering or, more likely, inadequate intelligence analysis. Even worse, it was an example of the prosecutor's failure to understand that Reilly's schema of the event differed from his own, that they had different uses and understandings of "know," "disposed of," and "the means of ascertaining what happened," and the prosecutor's failure of his responsibility to request clarification when he didn't understand what Reilly was saying.

SECTION IV

Perjury charges across languages and cultures

Since the late 1960s, considerable interest has arisen concerning the problems of non-native English speakers in legal contexts that require court interpreters (Berk-Seligson 1990, 2009; Hale 2004). However good it is to see an awakening sensitivity to the social needs and rights of linguistic and cultural minorities, most of the work in this area has been limited to non-native speakers whose lack of English ability is so clear and obvious that interpreters are considered an absolute necessity for the administration of justice. Although courts in the United States continue to struggle as they deal with such matters, gradual progress seems to be taking place.

In his informative book, *Forensic Linguistics* (2003, 200–227), John Gibbons describes the language problems of various disadvantaged speakers, including children, indigenous minorities, the deaf, and second-language speakers, who found themselves entangled in legal matters. In one case description, Gibbons discusses an interrogation of a young Tongan-Australian, whose ability in English was severely limited. His examination was conducted in English, but he was unable to represent himself adequately because he lacked the language competence that native English speakers have. This was exacerbated by the specialized lexicon and syntactic complexity that the police used when they questioned him. Similar problems of second-language speakers in lawyer-client interviews have been discussed by Pauwels, D'Argaville, and Eades (1992 & 2008), and by deaf people in Ceil Lucas's *Language and the Law in Deaf Communities* (2003).

Far less frequently considered are the problems of second-language users who have learned English rather well by the time they run into judicial or law enforcement problems. They may give the appearance of being fully competent speakers, but often, like most second-language users, they continue to have nagging difficulties based on the transfer of their native language lexicon, grammar, pragmatics, and discourse style to the required and expected system of English. This problem is illustrated in different ways by the two perjury cases described in chapters 9 (a Filipino-American physician) and 10 (a Hawaiian Creole–speaking union representative).

Chapter 9 reprises John Gumperz's description of a case that took place some three decades ago. A U.S.-trained and certified Filipino physician, whose native languages were Aklan and Tagalog, was trained in a U.S. medical school and was then assigned to a naval hospital in California, where he ran afoul of the perjury law largely because of his almost indistinguishable (except to Gumperz) lack of native English competence.

Chapter 10 describes the perjury case of a union representative whose native language was Hawaiian Creole but who spoke English rather well and was convicted of perjury for questionable reasons. His schema about the requirements of the grand jury speech event caused him to be extremely cautious as he responded to the prosecutor's questions, a cautiousness that led to his conviction.

It's one thing to charge native English speakers with perjury, but quite another when these speakers are unfamiliar with the English that they are expected to process and understand. In such cases, the language used by law enforcement officers or prosecutors can be interpreted very differently from the way they may have intended it and the answers they get can suggest that the target or witness understands things in a different way. When this happens, we are several steps away from the issues in the earlier noted *Bronston* case, because the speakers may not intend to provide partial or irrelevant responses.

Chapter 10 offers a very different account of language variation issues found in evidence of perjury. In this case it was the undercover police who used a vernacular dialect of English that was troublesome for the target, a lawyer, to understand as he interviewed them. This case reversed the production of language interference from that of the witness to that of the investigator.

(9)
A doctor charged with perjury

Linguist John Gumperz described a case from the late 1970s in which a Filipino physician who was a native speaker of Aklan and was fluent Tagalog and English was charged with perjury (Gumperz 1990, 163–195). The doctor had learned English well enough to graduate from the University of California and then to pass his medical boards in the United States. He was practicing medicine as an emergency room doctor at a Navy Hospital in Southern California when two parents rushed their young daughter into the emergency room, saying that the girl had been overexposed to the sun. The doctor observed the girl carefully and reported first- and second-degree burns on her upper torso, noting that the child was alert, had no respiratory distress, and that her symptoms comported with a normal sunburn case. He recommended that the parents take their child home, administer plenty of fluids, and bring her back to the hospital for once-a-day treatments for her burns until they healed. Important to this case, he didn't feel that he needed to enquire whether the parents had inflicted the burns on the child intentionally.

Six hours later, after this doctor had gone off his shift, the girl's parents brought her back to the same emergency room, where the new attending doctor determined that the child was suffering from severe dehydration and was covered with third-degree burns that were much more serious than originally diagnosed. The child's condition was so severe in fact that she died while being transported to another hospital that had the proper burn care facilities.

By the time the first doctor who saw the girl returned to work the next day, it had become apparent that her burns had been inflicted intentionally. An FBI agent was on the scene and, among his other duties, he interviewed this doctor for about fifteen minutes, taking very brief notes—twelve brief handwritten statements that eventually became part of the evidence in a subsequent first-degree murder trial of the child's stepfather.

The doctor was called as a witness for the prosecution in this trial, and that's when his legal problems began. He testified that the symptoms he observed during his emergency room examination did not indicate enough severity to merit hospitalization and that he had no reason to disbelieve the parents' explanation of sunburn. The attending nurse fully supported the doctor's testimony.

Eventually, a jury convicted the stepfather of murder, but this did not end the story because shortly afterward the prosecution reviewed the doctor's testimony and charged him with perjury. The government's claim was based on what the doctor had testified at trial compared with a later written FBI report that contained much more information than he included in his twelve brief items or notes that the agent had made during his fifteen-minute interview with the doctor on the day following the girl's death. This much-expanded police report said that during the child's second visit to the hospital, medical personnel reported that they suspected that the doctor's earlier treatment was negligent and, more astounding, that the doctor had admitted to them that he suspected child abuse all along but found it difficult to confront parents with this unless he had positive evidence that would make him 100% certain. The words "positive evidence" had appeared in the agent's brief notes in his initial interview with the doctor, but not in the context in which doctor claimed that he originally said these words. But now these words became the basis of the perjury charge that claimed the doctor testified contrary to what he originally told the other medical personnel.

At the doctor's perjury trial, the dead girl's mother, who had since divorced the stepfather, testified for the prosecution, even though she had said nothing about her husband's abuse to the doctor when she brought her daughter to the hospital. The FBI agent now testified that during his fifteen-minute interview the doctor had admitted his suspicion of child abuse, even though his handwritten notes reported nothing about this. Supporting the doctor's diagnosis, pediatric specialists familiar with child abuse testified that it is not uncommon for third-degree burns to appear on the skin several hours after exposure. The specialists testified that there were no compelling reasons to counter the doctor's original diagnosis. It should be noted that the doctor was not a seasoned pediatrician, and he was not familiar with child abuse because it is said not to exist in his native Philippines. It was also reported that there is no word for child abuse in Tagalog.

SECOND-LANGUAGE INTERFERENCE AND TRANSFER

The legal issue came down to which one was telling the truth: the Filipino-American doctor or the American FBI agent. Since one of the lawyers for the doctor noticed that the doctor's language had something "funny" about it, he called on Gumperz to see if he could figure out what this was and whether his analysis might help explain why the prosecution thought this was perjury. The defense recognized many discrepancies between the agent's handwritten notes and the later, much more detailed FBI report of the interview. Clearly it contained several after-the-fact new interpretations. But the problem this creates can be hard to prove, especially when there is an apparent public predisposition to convict negligent doctors along with a predictable public sympathy for children who are abused. Making things worse, it was hard for lawyers to explain communicative dissonance as a way of defending a doctor whose English seemed almost perfect, whether non-native or not. Since this looked like the job for language analysis, the defense attorney should be complimented for recognizing his need for linguistic help.

Gumperz began his analysis with a linguist's logical assumption, based on much research evidence, that there could be interference and transfer from the doctor's native language to his second language. He knew that if the defense would bring up the issue of comprehensibility in court, the prosecution could point to places in the doctor's testimony where he didn't use these odd grammatical features consistently or they would possibly claim that the doctor was merely pretending to have language problems. It is not clear from Gumperz's article whether the defense countered this claim with the logical response of linguists—that variability exists in virtually all language use, whether or not it is used by non-native speakers. But, good linguist that he is, Gumperz focused on the empirical language evidence that was available to him: the agent's brief on-the-scene notes, the later written, more detailed FBI report, the verbatim transcripts of the doctor's earlier testimony in the murder trial of the girl's stepfather, and his own informal tape-recorded conversation with the doctor, which he conducted in order to determine and better understand the doctor's language competence.

Gumperz discovered that the linguistic oddities in the doctor's testimony increased sharply when he discussed more cognitively complex topics, as when the prosecutor asked him to describe the academic content of the courses he took in medical school. These same features appeared much less frequently in the simple narratives that the prosecutor asked him to produce. In contrast with his short narrative answers to questions requiring temporal sequences of events, he gave long, complex, and sometimes confusing answers to questions that required him to recall several separate incidents that exemplify a single theme, to locate each incident in time, to show

how they relate to each other, and to tie them together in a cohesive sequence. This type of response required him to use conjunctions, pronouns, noun and verb complements, connectors, and qualifiers, all of which illustrated the "funny" language that his lawyer had noticed but didn't know how to identify or describe.

Among the potentially diagnostic features that Gumperz found in the doctor's complex topics were these odd examples of his grammar and lexicon:

- That's the standard that were lectured on for usually first- and second-degree burns.
- As far as the actual management.
- Secondary again it could be a foreign body.
- It could also have secondary to fluids.
- These were cases that have to be hospitalized. We don't have a chance to.

Gumperz also found that the doctor commonly switched topics in mid-sentence. Importantly, since the doctor seemed unaware that what he said might not be clear to those who heard him, he did not attempt to clarify his own sentence oddities. Gumperz concluded that the doctor was unconsciously using the style of English used by Filipino-English bilinguals, triggered by the required interview context and derived from Tagalog or Aklan. Gumperz also noticed that Tagalog has a system of aspectual distinctions and tense that is not marked in verbs the way it is in English. This caused the doctor to answer some past-tense questions with the present tense, intensified in those parts of the interview where the prosecutor's questions required more cognitively complex answers:

Q: Would you say that the two of you *were* good friends?
A: I would say that we *are* good friends

. . .

Q: Then am I to understand that you really *were not aware* at that time . . . ?
A: *I'm not aware.*

. . .

Q: . . . did you feel that the cause of the injuries *was* sunburn?
A: I *still feel* it was due to sunburn.

This last answer, using "still feel," makes it illogically appear that the doctor continued to believe that the cause was sunburn even though he knew full well that later it had been medically determined otherwise, to the extent that it contradicted what he had said at trial even after he learned the real cause.

The doctor's difficulties with negative questions, as well as the prosecutor's problems of understanding his answers, are illustrated briefly here:

Q: It's the testimony of the Lt. Commander that you did attend the briefing.
A: Yes.
Q: You did attend it?
A: No.
Q: Why didn't you attend that lecture?

This exchange is confusing, unless one takes into consideration the English skills of the doctor, who wanted to be accurate and truthful but was in a speech event context where he knew that he needed to weigh every word. The doctor's "yes" led the prosecutor to think that the doctor was agreeing that he did attend the briefing. But, his "yes" here agrees only that the Lt. Commander had testified that the doctor attended the meeting. A smore competent English speaker would have said, "That is not accurate" or "The Lt. Commander is wrong," or something to this effect. By his third question, we can see that the prosecutor finally understood the doctor's first two confusing answers.

In another exchange we see the following:

Q: What steps did you take to determine that?
A: When the child came, I initially examined the patient and I noted the moistness of the tongue, sunken eyes, the skin color, and everything was okay.
Q: Are you suggesting that there were no sunken eyes?
A: No.
Q: I think we better slow down a little bit more and make sure the record, did you observe sunken eyes?
A: No.

Despite his statement, "everything was okay," the doctor's language ability failed him here. He should have said "no sunken eyes" and "normal skin color" but in his mind he was going through the list of symptoms indicating third-degree burns. It confused the prosecutor enough to request clarification.

It's also apparent that the prosecutor had trouble understanding what the doctor was trying to say in the following:

Q: You indicated that you knew you had to report a suspected child abuse, isn't that correct?
A: To report? No.
Q: Okay, let's go back. My understanding of the witness's testimony is that he was doing a consultation on a case of child abuse that he suspected. A medical consultation. Not reporting requirements.

CULTURAL INTERFERENCE

To this point, Gumperz had identified at least some of the sources of the government's possible misunderstanding of what the doctor was saying, along with the way his native Tagalog influenced his handling of verb tenses and other lexical and grammatical forms. He also learned that the doctor's sensitivity to inference was culturally influenced because of his life in the Philippines, which made him unfamiliar with the fact that children could be abused. Like most of us, the doctor relied on his past experience (his schema) when he dealt with new situations. When asked if there were any other sources of burns that he's observed, the doctor went into a long report of the way houses in his native country do not have natural gas or electric cooking, saying:

> A: . . . most of the patients that go there [to the hospital] are the poverty-stricken patients, unlike you going to a medical center it's usually the middle class who go where you don't have this problem.

This utterance is confusing. We can't tell whether he is comparing poverty-stricken patients with middle-class patients or whether his point is how hospitals in the Philippines compare with hospitals in America. Part of his problem is his use of "unlike." If we attach it to the preceding clause, the expression is confusing. If we attach it to the following clause, it could make a bit more sense. The clause does not tell us exactly what the doctor is trying to compare. In Tagalog, the "unlike" clause ties together two clauses but in that language the two clauses are considered to be independent. There is nothing quite like this in English.

In Tagalog, there are contextualization conventions that appear to be transported into English when Filipinos speak, especially in inter-clause syntax with ellipsis. The doctor's English was acceptable in much of his testimony, but when the prosecutor challenged his testimony and the doctor had to justify himself with precise definitions, no matter how good his skills in English were, they proved to be not entirely satisfactory. It is well known that stress and complexity can seriously affect the language proficiency of speakers of any second language—or first language for that matter.

INTONATION

There are many other aspects of Gumperz's analysis that are too complex to go into here, including the way the doctor used the intonation of Tagalog in his oral testimony. In his book, Gumperz describes Tagalog intonation as having "a prosodic monotony which at times makes it difficult for listeners relying on American English [listening] strategies to determine what is being emphasized and where the segment is going" (191). Grammatical presuppositions can interact with prosodic signals, also leading to misunderstandings. An example in the doctor's case was an enlarged photo offered by the prosecution, showing the grisly condition of the girl when she was brought to the emergency room the second time. The prosecutor introduced the photo, knowing full well that no corresponding photo existed for the time when the girl was brought to the hospital the first time:

Q: Assume that it is one set of burns, you saw the picture—
A: Yeah but uh—
Q: Now if you saw that picture at the time at twelve o'clock, there's no question about it that it is a case of child abuse—
A: But I did not have nothing to cover up because I did not see those pictures, I mean those extensiveness of burn at twelve o'clock.
Q: Right.

> A: Now if they assume that burn or those burns were there at twelve o'clock, and I missed it, and that's their theory that they're working on, therefore I was, uh covered myself to commit perjury but the fact is that I did not see it, as confirmed by the nurses and the physical therapist, what is my motive?

The prosecutor appears to have been offering a badly phrased hypothetical here, which the doctor, under stressful conditions, did not handle well. He seems to try to counter and convey that there was no photo taken when he was there earlier when the girl was brought in at six o'clock and that this photo was taken at the child's second visit, at twelve o'clock. But his "therefore" seems to indicate that he's saying that he tried to cover this up by committing perjury. Under great stress, his otherwise rather good English fails him and he can't quite get his English right when he tries to explain this.

To test how confusing this passage was, Gumperz played it to a number of native American speakers, all of whom thought that the photo was taken at 6 o'clock, not at the true time it was actually taken, which was at 12 o'clock. It's hard to know what the jurors thought, but it's likely that they could have gotten the same impression.

This case illustrates a number of factors that need to be considered when the prosecution charges a non-native speaker with perjury, even one with apparently good surface language skills.

1. Police procedure factors:

As in any criminal case, the prosecution's procedures and evidence has to be evaluated. Was the investigator's fifteen-minute interview with the doctor adequate? Were his brief, twelve-item, handwritten notes adequate, complete, and accurate? We will never know in this case. It would have been far better for the investigator to have tape-recorded this interview so that his notes could be checked for accuracy against the more detailed FBI report that he eventually submitted. The recent tape-recording efforts of some law enforcement agencies in the effort to assure that their interviews are conducted properly and reported accurately have been viewed as an advantage for law enforcement, because audio or video tapes preserve exactly what happened and validate the accuracy of the interviewers' notes and summary reports. Interestingly, they also reduce unnecessary arguments and conflict at trial, saving valuable resources and time for both the prosecution and the defense. In short, the intelligence gathering here left much to be desired.

2. Prosecutorial procedure factors:

It would seem logical that when a witness is having a difficult time answering questions in a way that comports with the expected use of English grammar and discourse conventions, the questioner might be wise to simplify, request clarification, or otherwise employ competent strategies to get at the truth. Lawyers love to ask hypothetical questions, especially when things don't seem to be going their way in the courtroom exchange. Such questions are difficult for even native speakers to deal with, but asking non-natives hypotheticals can have consequences that can be very unfair.

Furthermore, prosecutors are at the top layer of the intelligence analysis process. When questionable evidence is given them, it's their duty to send the data-gathering investigators back for more reliable evidence. In retrospect, even the police must consider their fifteen-minute interview with the doctor grossly inadequate, especially since Gumperz notes that this brief interview was interrupted several times when the doctor was called into other emergency room cases. Then there is the matter of the agent's twelve-item notes, which did not always comport with the eventual FBI report of the incident that was used against the doctor. And we don't need to even mention the fact that the medical personnel at the original treatment scene supported the doctor's decision about the girl's condition when she first came to the emergency room, and that the pediatric specialist testified that serious aspects of the girl's condition can take several hours to present themselves. This would indicate that the doctor had no particular reason to suspect child abuse. He was truthful in admitting this, so the prosecutor went after the alleged conflict between what he was reported to have told the agent in the brief interview and what he said in his testimony at the murder trial of the stepfather. One can only wonder at the prosecutor's motivation, especially when it was based on the agent's apparently shaky memory of what he could recall from his hasty interview of the non-native speaker of English who was stressed and shocked to learn of the terrible chain of events.

3. Culture factors:

A non-native speaker whose culture does not experience this type of crime and whose language is said to not even have a word for child abuse is not likely to be consciously aware of it or to be on the lookout for it. Gumperz also noted that the Filipino culture is predisposed to avoid interfering with the closeness of family bonds and the extent to which they reveal such matters to outsiders. The doctor did not probe the parents about whether they had committed child abuse for two reasons: (1) there was no indication of it when he saw the patient, and (2) because even doing so would run counter his cultural assumption about not probing into the family affairs of others.

4. Language factors:

As noted above, a major consideration is the transfer of grammatical forms, lexicon, and discourse style from the doctor's native language to his second language. When language interference causes communication confusion, the courts might be expected to take this carefully into consideration. In addition, this case shows clearly that when two different units of time are involved, it is extremely important to be exactly accurate about what was done, seen, and reported in each of the two clearly identified time units and to not mix them up. The critical time units here were six hours apart. A non-native speaker whose first language distinguishes verb tenses differently from English is especially vulnerable in such cases. Likewise, the doctor's lack of awareness about whether or not he was being understood disadvantaged him by leaving his less-than-clear statements hanging, with no opportunity to employ a native speaker's ability to provide discourse clarification.

(10)
A union representative charged with perjury

Steven Suyat was a second-generation Filipino who was born and raised on the backwater Hawaiian island of Molokai, population of about twelve thousand at that time, where many of the inhabitants of the island worked in the cane fields or factories. Suyat was in a class of about a hundred students who graduated from the island's only high school. He spoke both Hawaiian Creole and Hawaiian Pidgin English. As a very young man he decided on carpentry for his life work and after about seven years his hard work, skills, and integrity were recognized and the Hawaii Carpenters Union promoted him to business representative on the island of Maui.

In 1981, the carpenters union grew at odds with a certain non-unionized general contractor because that contractor was not paying his workers the rate that matched the prevailing standard wage. When the contractor refused to pay the prevailing rate, the union conducted legal informational picketing at all of the contractor's building sites. The contractor was furious about this and filed unfair labor practices charges with the National Labor Relations Board (NLRB). The conflict was about whether the picketing was actually informational or whether it was an effort to force the contractor to agree to the union's collective-bargaining agreement. The NLRB then followed its standard negotiation procedures. The union's business agents filed affidavits to set forth their position on the matter and the dispute was settled before any litigation took place.

But the union's problems did not end there. About eighteen months later, the U.S. District Attorney's office became suspicious of the affidavit statements made by the union's business agents. Two of these agents were suspected of making false statements about the informational nature of the picketing and were called to testify in a series of grand jury hearings. Unbeknownst to them, the contractor had covertly tape-recorded his conversations with these two business agents, Ralph Torres and William Nishibayashi, and had turned over the tapes to the U.S. District Attorney's office. On these tapes, the two men revealed that the picketing was not for informational purposes but instead, it was carried out to pressure the contractor's carpenters to unionize.

Based largely on these tape recordings, Torres and Nishibayashi were tried and convicted. Suyat was not charged in this case, but the prosecutor called him as a witness against his two fellow union representatives at their trial. Suyat testified at the grand jury hearings and seemed to have emerged unscathed, probably because he was not a party to the secret tape-recordings and he had nothing to do with the illegal picketing.

Apparently, however, the prosecutor was not satisfied that Suyat was totally innocent in the picketing incident. After reviewing Suyat's trial testimony, the prosecutor indicted him on seven charges of perjury. Because the perjury charges made against him had nothing to do with the major issues of the trial of his two colleagues, a skeptical observer might think that the prosecutor was overly eager to find something upon which to convict even more union representatives. Failing at this, the prosecutor charged Suyat with seven counts of perjury that grew out of his grand jury testimony. In it, Suyat was alleged to have made false statements about what can only be considered ancillary, relatively minor matters. Recognizing this, Suyat's attorney called on me to contribute whatever linguistic expertise I could provide, in the hope that it might help his client.

Four of the seven perjury counts declared that Suyat had made false statements when he said, and then repeated three more times, that he did not know what the word "organizing" means. Two of the charges were that Suyat made a false statement when twice he said that he did not know what the word, "scab," means. The seventh and last perjury charge was based on Suyat's answer that he did not recall anything he overheard in a conversation between the union's head, Walter Kupau, and Torres. In contrast, when his defense attorney asked him the very same question on cross-examination, Suyat recalled that he thought Kupau may have told Torres that he had received a letter from Honolulu.

COUNT 7: DIFFERENT MEANINGS OF "RECALL"

When the prosecutor at the grand jury hearing had Suyat on the witness stand, this exchange took place:

Prosecutor:	Do you recall him [the union head, Walter Kupau] ever having a conversation with Ralph Torres?
Suyat:	Yes.
Prosecutor:	Do you recall when those were?
Suyat:	No.
Prosecutor:	Do you recall what he said to Ralph Torres?
Suyat:	No.

It seems clear that Suyat had some memory of a conversation between Kupau and Torres, but he couldn't recall when this conversation took place or what they said to each other. But three hours later, when his defense attorney cross-examined Suyat about this, the following exchange took place:

Defense attorney:	Do you recall what Mr. Torres said in response to this?
Suyat:	I believe Mr. Torres, I think, told him that he received a letter from Honolulu and everything is respond back to the Honolulu office, to Mr. Kupau.

On the surface at least, it would appear that Suyat produced contradictory testimony. His two statements about the same subject were inconsistent, but the question is whether this amounts to perjury.

DECEPTION OR MEMORY PROBLEMS?

It is not difficult to understand how a person's memory can be imperfect. We often don't recall something at one time, but then suddenly remember it at another time. What is significant about this charge, however, is that Suyat would gain absolutely no advantage by reporting his newly discovered memory of this conversation the second time the question was asked. It is much more likely that a liar would try to preserve the authenticity of his earlier non-memory, because giving two different answers to the same question would certainly look suspicious. In addition, it is reasonable to believe that a missing memory of a person under the extreme stress of courtroom testimony can be refreshed, especially when the questioner is not the adversary. Or it may be that Suyat's defense lawyer knew or suspected strongly that his client should have recalled this conversation and so he simply gave Suyat the opportunity to repair his earlier memory lapse. Those of us who experience the tension when being examined by a hostile adversary in a formal court setting can easily sympathize with Suyat, and those of us who have served as expert witnesses in criminal trials can easily understand that count 7 of the prosecutor's indictment was a real stretch here.

And what are we to make of Suyat's stumbling "I think" and "I believe" in his response? Was Suyat more comfortable and perhaps saving face by answering his friendly lawyer about what he stumblingly remembered had happened than to face the risk of being tentative, incomplete, or inaccurate to the prosecutor in this formal speech event? Who would he fear most? Given the consequences of being inaccurate, or even slightly inaccurate, in a setting that demands accuracy, many people are quick to say "I don't know" or "I don't recall." It's safer to say this than to offer fuzzy memories or sheer speculations. Lawyers conventionally advise witnesses to do this. To test this, I examined the rest of his testimony and found that Suyat:

- requested clarification of the prosecutor's questions twenty-five times
- qualified his answers with "I think" or "I believe" thirty-two times
- corrected the prosecutor's overgeneralization one time.

If Suyat requested clarification, qualified his responses, and even went so far as to correct the prosecutor's overgeneralization this often, we can ask why he didn't do so when asked about his memory of the conversation between Kupau and Torres. One possible answer is that he genuinely didn't remember it at the time he was asked, but then later recovered some dim memories about it. Memory lapses happen to us all, but they hardly fall into the category of perjury, especially when they are almost immediately corrected.

THE MEANING OF "RECALL"

I also wondered how the prosecutor's questions might have affected Suyat's answers. In his direct examination the prosecutor asked Suyat to "recall" sixteen times, whereas the defense attorney's questions consistently used "remember." It's at least possible that Suyat, being careful and conscientious and realizing that this speech event called for total accuracy and truth, inferred that "recall" requires precision of memory that he didn't, or couldn't call up, while "remember" allowed him to give qualified responses such as "I think" and "I believe." Common dictionary definitions don't offer much help for this distinction, but the synonym given in *Merriam-Webster's Collegiate Dictionary* entry for "remember" says:

> REMEMBER implies a keeping in memory that may be effortless or unwilled... RECALL suggests an effort to bring back to mind and often to recreate in speech.

Garner's *A Dictionary of Modern Legal Usage* (1995) offers a similar distinction:

> To *remember* is to recall what is ready at hand in one's memory. To *recollect* is to find something stored further back in the mind.

CONFLICT IN THE MEANINGS OF OTHER WORDS

Opponents in trials sometimes don't understand each other's word meanings. Suyat's experience was no exception. In other parts of his testimony, it was clear that the prosecutor used "accurate" to mean "true," while Suyat's responses showed that he understood this word to mean "specific" or "complete." When the prosecutor used "approve" to mean "knowing about" or "agreeing with," Suyat's answers showed that he understood this to mean "officially endorse" or "counter sign." Even the prosecutor's simple word, "friend," triggered Suyat to respond with the meaning of "work associate" and the prosecutor's "caught" (meaning prevent from crossing the picket line) to Suyat meant "note the exact times the picket lines were crossed." The difference between "recall" and "remember" was only one of their lexical trains passing in the night.

At least part of Suyat's problem relates to the fact that trials are conducted under a strict set of conversational rules that are well known by lawyers and judges but can turn out to be a mire of trickery for even that mythical *reasonable person* that law loves to cite. Trials can have serious communication breakdowns when the words that are used are understood very differently by the participants, even when their language skills are roughly equivalent. But when there is a larger gap in language competence between participants, as this case evidenced, the chance of achieving conversational synchrony and agreement on the meaning of words moves even farther apart. In such cases, the participants can appear to be inconsistent or perhaps even to be committing perjury.

Although the seventh charge illustrates some of the cross-cultural problems of a less-than-fluent English speaker who is suddenly plopped into a very different courtroom culture, the first six perjury charges even better illustrate the linguistic problems faced by a witness whose English skills are skimpy.

COUNTS 1 THROUGH 4: DIFFERENT MEANINGS OF "ORGANIZE"

Counts 1 through 4 related to the duties of Suyat and his colleagues at the union, all noted by the prosecutor while Suyat testified for him in the government's criminal cases against Torres and Nishibayashi. At one point, the prosecutor asked him about "organizing" contractors:

Count 1:
Prosecutor: And one of the jobs of the business agent is to organize non-union contractors, is that right?
Suyat: No.
Count 2:
Prosecutor: So no part of your job is to organize contractors?
Suyat: No.
Count 3:
Prosecutor: And so no part of Mr. Nishibayashi's job is to organize contactrors?
Suyat: That's right.
Count 4:
Prosecutor: And no part of Mr. Torres' job is to organize contractors?
Suyat: That's right.

It doesn't take a linguistic expert witness to figure out the syntax here:

name (subject) organize (verb) contractors (object).

It can only be assumed that the prosecutor meant something different here, such as:

name (subject) organize (verb) carpenters who work for contractors (object + modifying noun clause).

Perhaps many would understand the sentence the way the prosecutor probably meant it. But Suyat did not. He knew that the job of union business agents was to organize *workers,* but not to organize *contractors.* Suyat carefully weighed every word the prosecutor said in his questions. He knew that his education, culture, and English skills didn't match those of the well-educated prosecutor, and he knew that he had to tell the truth at all times and to not become trapped by trick questions. So when the prosecutor put forth what seemed to Suyat to be an inaccurate definition of the work of union business agents, he knew that he had to answer truthfully. What could be more logical than to answer that union business agents *do not* organize contractors?

SCHEMA AND THE SPEECH EVENT

Then why didn't Suyat simply correct the prosecutor's statement? To answer this question, we need to understand the wide gap in status that he felt (and most of the rest of us feel) when we find ourselves in powerless contexts like a courtroom, where everything is controlled by judges and lawyers, where the language is new and strange, where the procedures are those of a very different culture, and where you can get into deep trouble unless you weigh every word carefully. This speech event requires witnesses to follow the maxim of informativeness and answer only that which they are asked, nothing more, nothing less. In their schema of the entire speech event, they have to be alert for questions they don't expect. They know that language matters here, so they have to follow the rules, some of which they may not know or understand. Their schema also tells them that the prosecutor is an intelligent person with an important job. He knows what he is doing. Maybe he really believed that unions organize contractors. Even though Suyat had never heard of this, who was he to doubt the powerful prosecutor's words that organizing contractors might be taking place somewhere. For all Suyat knew, it might even be true that some unions actually do organize contractors. He thought the best strategy was to tell the truth here: "No, our job is not to organize contractors."

REQUESTING CLARIFICATION

We might also ask why Suyat did not ask the prosecutor to clarify his question. The answer is the same as above. How could he, a relatively uneducated man, even phrase such a request? The word, "organize," wasn't particularly unclear. To him the question sounded more like something the prosecutor knew but that Suyat didn't know, and maybe he even should have known. He didn't feel he could challenge the prosecutor and ask, "do you really mean organize workers?" It would be dangerously face threatening to the prosecutor if Suyat told him that he had made a stupid mistake. Even saying, "I don't understand your question" would seem like criticizing the prosecutor for not wording it properly. Better to take the option that the prosecutor really meant "organize contractors."

Dictionaries, such as *Merriam-Webster's Collegiate Dictionary* agree with Suyat:

> contractor: 1. one that contracts or is a party to a contract: as
> a: one that contracts to perform work or supplies
> b: one that contracts to erect buildings.

Whether or not the urban Honolulu jurors realized it, this count presented them with the task of dealing with two conflicting sets of intentions. It is ironic that in his effort to be respectful and scrupulously accurate, Suyat was convicted of perjury.

COUNTS 5 AND 6: DIFFERENT WAYS OF DEFINING "SCAB"

Counts 5 and 6 were also extracted from Suyat's testimony at the trial of his two union colleagues, when he thought the prosecutor asked him to give a definition of the word "scab." These counts reveal a still-different linguistic aspect of Suyat's testimony. These counts relate to Suyat's schema of the role or stance that the prosecutor's questions expected him to take in his answers:

Count 5:	
Prosecutor:	What does the word "scab" mean?
Suyat:	I have no recollection.
Count 6:	
Prosecutor:	You don't know what the word "scab" means?
Suyat:	No.

As a union representative, Suyat surely knew and used the word "scab." Unions use it all the time to refer to workers who won't join the union, to refer to union members who don't honor picket lines during labor strikes, to describe non-union workers hired to replace striking union members, and to refer to employees who agree to work for less than the union rate. In fact, this is how dictionaries define the word. So why would Suyat say that he didn't know what "scab" means here?

SOCIOLINGUISTIC SCHEMA, ROLE, AND STANCE IN AN INTERACTION

To answer this question, we need to consider how Suyat's schema of his own role and stance in this speech event. He quickly needed to interpret whether the prosecutor wanted him to (1) give a dictionary definition, (2) give a personal definition, or (3) give an informal definition that he may have heard someone else give.

The prosecutor gave no clear indication that he wanted Suyat's personal definition of "scab." He asked, "what does the word 'scab' mean?" Being a dutiful citizen and desperately trying to comply with what he thought was wanted in the unfamiliar and terrifying context of the courtroom, Suyat assumed that he should answer with what he thought the question required: a dictionary definition. He felt inadequate to remember any good dictionary definition that he may or may not have ever seen. He had "no recollection" of such a definition and he was too frightened about being wrong to venture giving one of his own. Maybe the prosecutor actually understood this because in his follow-up question he referred to Suyat's notebook, which, along with many other union documents, also had been placed in evidence:

Prosecutor:	So you don't remember what you meant by it when you put it down here?
Suyat:	Well, yeah—
Prosecutor:	Thank you. I have no further questions, your honor.

The prosecutor used two familiar trial lawyer strategies here: the hit-and-run strategy and the strategy of ignoring the rules of English concord.

THE PROSECUTOR'S HIT-AND-RUN STRATEGY

This conversational strategy is common in the courtroom, used by prosecutors and defense attorneys alike. Elsewhere I have described this as a conversational strategy used by undercover law enforcement officers in cases involving covert tape-recorded evidence (Shuy 2005). In such cases, agents sometimes introduce a topic that is potentially damaging to a target, then change the subject quickly to something benign, essentially encouraging the target to focus on the benign topic and ignore the damaging topic, especially when the target's response might have included exculpatory statements. When an exchange is recorded on tape, quickly changing the subject prevents later listeners, such as juries, from hearing whatever the target might have said. The courtroom procedure is usually not tape-recorded, but the power of the prosecutor to control the way language is used enables the hit-and-run strategy to work pretty much in the same way in courtroom examinations of witnesses.

Lawyers have been known to suddenly break off their questioning when they get an answer they really like. The sole and absolute power they have in the question/answer routine required by the courts gives them a great advantage here. For example, a witness has to answer a yes/no question with either a yes or a no, whether or not the response can or will provide the full and accurate picture. "Yes, but..." answers are quickly blocked by the lawyer's "thank you," which stops the respondent cold in his tracks. Suyat's "well, yeah" ended with rising intonation, showing that he had more to say on the subject if only he were allowed to say it. From his perspective, it was not the end of his turn of talk. He had something else to say that would explain his answer, which was likely to be, yes he used the word, "scab," he had a clear understanding of its meaning, and he wanted to explain himself further. We can't know this for sure, of course, but the linguistic clues certainly point strongly in that direction.

THE PROSECUTOR'S STRATEGY OF IGNORING ENGLISH CONCORD RULES

The second conversational strategy by the prosecutor was to ignore the positive and negative concord rules of English (Huddleston and Pullum 2002, 847–48). If a speaker asks a question using positive words (with no negatives such as "not" or "never"), respondents who want to agree use positives in their answers. For example, if the question is, "Did that happen?" and the respondent wants to agree that it happened, the answer indicating agreement would be "yes." But if the question is, "That never happened?" the response of agreement would be "no." Positively worded questions are agreed to with positively worded answers and negatively worded questions are agreed to with negatively worded answers. The reverse answers are given when the respondent wants to disagree. Concord is preserved both ways, but problems come up when speakers misunderstand or misuse the concord rules.

Here the prosecutor asked the question negatively ("you don't remember"), meaning that agreement with it would have to be conveyed with a negative, such as "no," meaning "I agree that I don't remember." But here Suyat didn't say this. His positive response, "Well, yeah," indicated he indeed *did* remember what he meant when he wrote "scab" in his notebook. In other words, although he didn't feel that he was able to give a dictionary definition of "scab" in counts 5 and 6, he certainly could give his personal definition when the prosecutor finally got around to contextualizing with Suyat's notebook. These two perjury charges might not have been made if Suyat had not been interrupted but, rather, was allowed to complete what his sense of English concord and sentence intonation suggested he was about to say.

One question we might ask is whether Suyat, who certainly was not an accomplished speaker of English, really had control of English positive and negative concord rules. The best evidence comes from the rest of his answers during his testimony, where it is clear he had learned to use these rules appropriately. One such example is:

Prosecutor:	But that never happened with regard to supplies or anything? He never wanted to put up the picket line just to stop supplies from coming in?
Suyat:	No, no, no.

Suyat's negative response said, in essence, "I agree that he never wanted to put up picket lines just to stop supplies from coming in." In this and in many other similar examples the prosecutor went right on, indicating that he accepted Suyat's ability to use English negative and positive concord rules appropriately. It seems odd that he didn't accept it this final time however.

Many people are justifiably convicted of perjury when the known and verifiable facts conflict with what the witnesses say. In Suyat's case, there were no facts associating him with the evidence that convicted his union associates, Torres and Nishibayashi. Suyat even had the unenviable task of being called as a prosecution witness against his fellow workers. So in order to convict Suyat, all that the prosecutor had to go on was his testimony before the grand jury. As can be seen here, he used his power and control over different meanings of words like "recall," his own unclear use of "organize," and his prosecutorial tricks about the meaning of "scab" to make it appear that Suyat had perjured himself. As for Suyat, his lower social status, his personal schema about the speech event, his extreme care in using his second language, and his recognition of his own powerlessness did him in. But the prosecutor can hardly be proud of the way this turned out.

SECTION V

Perjury cases with adequate intelligence analyses

The legal profession is steeped in the process of interpretation (Blakey 1993, vii). This is generally thought to be interpreting statutes in and by the courts, but interpretation begins much earlier than that, often when the intelligence is being gathered. Nor is the field of law alone in this. All professions, in fact all people, have to gather and interpret information daily. The best process is no different from the accepted procedures of science:

1. Define an important as-yet-unresolved problem.
2. Collect data relevant to the problem.
3. Organize that data in such a way that analysis can be made.
4. Analyze the data using the appropriate methods and tools.
5. Report the findings in a coherent way.

Intelligence analysts follow these same five steps. Law enforcement officers begin with a hypothesis, such as the possibility that a crime was committed. To test this hypothesis, they gather information, which could be anything relevant, including documents of various types, telephone records, and undercover tape-recordings. This is the intelligence gathering. The best intelligence gathering is focused rather than random, because this saves time, energy, and the embarrassment of pursuing the wrong suspects. Next, the analysts compare the already known evidence and facts with any newer information collected in the process that will either support or disconfirm their hypothesis. For example, they can compare known telephone records with newly gathered undercover tape-recordings. Finally, they use every tool available to analyze and interpret their findings. This step is the intelligence analysis.

Things can go wrong at any of these five steps. The hypothesis may be wrong, the intelligence gathering may prove faulty, the comparison stage may prove to be unsatisfactory, the data organization may be inept, and the analysis may not take advantage of the most useful and powerful available tools and procedures.

It is equally important to separate the functions of intelligence gathering from intelligence analysis. Intelligence gathering is the objective collecting of facts that may ultimately support or reject the analyst's hypothesis of guilt or innocence. Intelligence analysis is done by the prosecutor or district attorney after the non-advocacy intelligence has been scientifically and neutrally gathered. Impatient advocacy can have an unfortunate way of slipping in during the intelligence gathering, which can then lead to disastrous results for the eventual prosecution at trial.

The time has long passed when law enforcement and prosecution were isolated from the academic information that could help them. Today, for example, from the field of sociology they have available to them the contributions of interaction networks, attitudes, and loyalties. They have the ethnographic knowledge of anthropology about the structures and networks of criminal institutions, and they have the knowledge from economics about the way criminals use the marketplace. From psychology, they have psychological profiling research that helps them to determine the possible type of offender and to narrow down their lists of suspects. From political science, they can learn about how crime undermines government structures. From historians of organized crime, they can learn much about the rise and decline of such organizations, pointing to the facts of history to guide present and future investigations.

In the past three decades, we have also seen the rapid development and advancement of linguistics in the area of criminal and civil law. This is only natural, because most such cases take place in language. Although it may seem obvious to the field of law that sociology, anthropology, economics, psychology, and history can play a role in helping with legal issues, linguistics has had a harder time breaking into the process. Part of this problem may be the fault of linguists, who have simply not realized how fruitful the area of law can be for applications by their field. But another and perhaps more serious part of the problem is that lawyers and judges use language extremely well, making it less than obvious to them that linguistics has something useful to contribute. Many lawyers and judges also analyze language very well, contributing to their sense of self-confidence in their own linguistic abilities. But there is also an important difference, whether or not they realize it. Linguists have analytical tools and training that lawyers, even the best ones, do not usually possess. Linguists see patterns and features that are unseen by non-linguists, just as dentists see things in X-rays that are invisible to patients.

To recapitulate a bit, this book illustrates some of the ways linguists analyze perjury cases. Not all linguistic tools are used in each case, because the nature of the evidence in these cases did not always require the application of all of the tools in a linguist's tool kit. But together the perjury cases described in the preceding chapters have introduced and illustrated how these the tools were used, including the speech event, schema theory, topic and agenda analysis, the use of speech acts, contextual meaning, the cooperative principle, ambiguity identification and resolution, the recency principle, grammatical referencing, evidence of intentionality, questioning strategies, clarification efforts, concord rules, language and second-culture interference, deceptive language, and literal versus figurative truth.

The following three chapters take a different perspective. They celebrate cases in which adequate intelligence analysis prevented the conviction of people based on inadequate intelligence gathering.

Chapter 11 describes the case of a lawyer enmeshed in a sting operation in Kansas City, a victim of inadequate intelligence gathering. This did not deter the prosecution, however, from indicting him and bringing him to trial. The hero in this case was a wise judge, who recognized the inadequacy of law enforcement's intelligence gathering and the prosecutor's intelligence analysis and threw the case out because the prosecution had failed to convince him that a case of perjury could be made.

Chapter 12 explains why a case against a sitting U.S. senator never even reached the indictment stage, despite the daily media frenzy about it. In this case the prosecutor carefully reviewed the intelligence gathered but couldn't convince himself that a perjury case should be made against the senator.

Finally, chapter 13 describes the serious problems faced by a prosecutor who brought a perjury indictment against a very popular local priest. The district attorney wasn't sure that the intelligence had been properly analyzed. He believed that the case was very weak and hired linguists to analyze the language evidence before the trial even began. Based on the analysis of the language in evidence, the district attorney dismissed the charges before the case went to trial.

Because hypotheses of guilt are difficult to overcome, it was heroic for a judge, a district attorney, and a prosecutor in these three cases to admit that the language evidence did not support the indictments.

As noted earlier, when the intelligence analysis is carried out by experts, they find that best approach is to be objective, to be scientific, and to develop more than one hypothesis. When prosecutors develop a hypothesis of innocence, even when the suspect or defendant at first seems very guilty, they gain the benefit of having answers ready for the probable defense strategy before the trial even begins. It's always good to know your opponent's position and be well prepared for it. And sometimes, when carefully assessed, the prosecution's hypothesis of guilt is not as good as the defense's hypothesis.

(11)
An attorney's aborted charge of suborning perjury

Although the verb phrase, "to suborn," means inducing or procuring a person to commit an illegal act, its common legal meaning today has narrowed almost exclusively to procuring a person to commit perjury (Garner 2005). A person who is accused of suborning perjury is tried in pretty much the same way as a person accused of committing perjury. Since the result of the perjury or suborning of perjury usually results in a crime of fraud, the persons involved in the act are likely to be charged with fraud as well. Sometimes lawyers are accused of suborning (encouraging or procuring their clients to lie), and lawyer Donald Crow found himself in the middle of a sting operation of exactly this type.

Law enforcement's sting operations can extend to all types of professions, including lawyers. For example, in the late 1970s, U.S. postal inspectors were trying to stop the proliferating practice of fraudulent personal-injury claims in and around Kansas City. Various physicians were suspected of submitting false medical information, and various lawyers were suspected of helping their clients construct false claims. The intelligence gathering part of the operation was a sting scenario that sent undercover agents pretending to be working-class citizens to lawyers' offices wearing hidden microphones to tape-record their interactions with lawyers or even with other employees in lawyers' offices. In some cases, the agents also tape-recorded their telephone calls with lawyers or their staff.

The agents' undercover strategy was to tell the lawyers that they had received injuries from recent automobile accidents and, in order to get a monetary recovery, they wanted the attorneys to help them file claims for medical reimbursement or other compensation. Things got a bit tricky at this point, however, because in order to catch these lawyers in actual fraud, the agents were ethically or legally required to make it clear at some point that their targets understood that these claims were actually false. When this happens, honest lawyers would then tell their new clients that they couldn't do this because it was against the law. The requirement to be clear and unambiguous about the illegal nature of the enterprise, also in effect at the FBI for undercover stings (although not made public until 1984), made it somewhat difficult for agents to nab lawyers in this operation. The FBI called these requirements "safeguards," as reported to the Committee on the Judiciary of the U.S. House of Representatives by the then–Assistant Attorney General, Phillip Heymann:

> The second major safeguard followed in every undercover operation, is making clear and unambiguous to all concerned the illegal nature of any opportunity used as a decoy (1984, 36).

After the U.S. Postal Service saw that adhering to this guideline was making it difficult for them to capture the illegality in the act, they created a new scheme in which they selected African-American agents who were familiar with Vernacular African-American English and culture, who pretended to be potential accident clients. The resulting inarticulate and ignorant-sounding accounts of their claims required the attorneys to infer a great deal about what they were trying to say. It's the job of lawyers to piece together their client's fragmentary or inarticulately phrased reports to discover a narrative. So the agents, who used a language variety and culture that was less familiar to the listeners, made the lawyers' task of distinguishing between dishonesty and honest ignorance a bit more challenging as they tried to piece together the client's story and determine whether it was false or true. Those who came to understand that these accounts were bogus could either stop right there and usher the agents/clients out of their office, or they could go along with it dishonestly and collect their fees. Of course, if they went along with the story, they could also be caught in the sting operation. In this new scenario, however, the agents increased the possibility of capturing a crime as it was happening, whether or not it was real.

Some of the lawyers and doctors who were caught in this sting may well have been crooked, but the undercover agents' strategy often relied more on inference than on fact, and the recorded conversations were subject to careful linguistic analysis. I have no idea whether other cases were disputed, but I do know about the case in which agents, posing as an African-American couple, walked into attorney Donald Crow's office to try out this newly created sting scenario.

Donald Crow was one of the many lawyers caught in this Kansas City sting. His office was located in a storefront shopping mall area, and his fees tended toward the low end, as was common in that part of the urban community. His was one of those general practices that have no particular specialization and that attracted walk-in clients. Of necessity, the time he had to spend on cases had to be as brief as possible. He was exactly the type of lawyer who was a good prospect for this new scenario devised by this sting operation. It should also be noted that the Postal Service had no basis for seeking out Crow. Their agents followed the trolling-for-possible-suspects approach that also was commonly used by law enforcement in other areas, such as terrorism cases (Shuy 2010, 558–75).

Several physicians and attorneys were indicted in this undercover operation, and things seemed to be going rather well for the agents until they tried to snare Crow, who was shocked when he received his indictment for false statements and fraud. Shortly after this, his criminal attorney called me to see what I could find in the language data of Crow's case.

THE SPEECH EVENT

My first step was to try to define the speech event in which the data of this case fit. This speech event can be called something like "a legal claim for obtaining a monetary recovery." It is important to know the expected sequence and procedures that a lawyer follows in this type of speech event. If Crow skipped some required features, he might be subject to criticism. In my book, *Language Crimes* (1993, 150), I described some aspects of this case, including the structured speech event of an attorney's interview in an injury claim. The typical steps are:

1. to confirm that the accident occurred, when, where, and so on;
2. to confirm that medical treatment was received;
3. to confirm that the medical problem persists;
4. to prepare a contract and authorization for medical treatment;
5. to execute the claim; and finally,
6. to resolve the claim.

Some of the lawyers caught or under investigation in the Kansas City sting had failed in steps 1 to 3, because they didn't follow the proper procedures for identifying and confirming the alleged injuries. Crow tried hard to get the proper information from his clients, but this was no easy task with the agents who came to him for legal help.

My examination of the tape-recorded interviews showed that he had followed the proper speech-event sequence for obtaining a claim. The agents gave Crow a police report documenting their accident, reported seeing a specifically named doctor for their injuries, and said they were getting medical treatments twice a week from that physician. So Crow went to step 4 and prepared a contract for them that authorized the release of their medical records. Then he executed their claim, and about six months later he presented them with a check for their injuries. No good case against Crow could be made for his failure to follow the accepted procedures required in this speech event.

The tape-recorded evidence showed clearly that after the agents reported their accident, the first thing Crow said to the clients was, "Okay, let me tell you what it takes to get a recovery from an insurance carrier as a result of a car accident" (step 1). Crow then carefully explained that victims can't make a claim unless they have suffered some kind of injury, that they had to have expended money with a doctor (step 2), and that if there is no permanent injury, victims can recover only wages lost, medical expenses, and transportation costs to and from the doctor's office (step 3). To get beyond this, quoting what Crow said on the tape:

> You have to have permanency, continuing aggravation that goes beyond the treatment. In your instance, there is nothing you can recover because you obviously have no permanency. Just because you are in an accident doesn't mean you are entitled to some money.

With their specific answers in hand, Crow then executed the claim (step 4) and eventually presented them with a check for their claim (steps 5 and 6).

DIFFERENT AGENDAS

Nevertheless, the government believed that Crow's two early interviews with these clients formed the government's case against him. The lawyer's purpose in these interviews was to gather information about his clients, which contrasted with his clients' purpose, which was to gather information about Crow. Paradoxically, they both were interviewing each other at the same time with totally different agendas that made cooperation and clarity rather difficult.

THE SPEECH ACT OF A DIRECTIVE WITH CONDITIONALITY

The prosecutors claimed that in one part of the interview Crow was actually giving the clients directives. In doing so, the prosecutors overlooked the "if" in Crow's main clause that governed the three clauses that followed but did not repeat his "if." Crow was speaking conditionally, which is far from giving a directive:

> Crow: Well, *if* your injuries or the pain that you suffered reoccurs and you go to a doctor and he administers treatment for that part and he is definitive enough after that treatment to indicate that that pain will probably occur again and again and again, then you've got a recovery possibility.

There is only one written "if" in that long sentence, but its scope governs the rest of the clauses in that sentence. English grammar specifies that an initial "if clause" governs all following clauses unless they are specifically changed. His "if" is grammatically understood also when he does not include it in:

"(if) you go to a doctor," "and (if) he administers," and "and (if) it is definite enough."

Therefore, his speech act was not a directive telling the clients what to do; he was using the speech act of advising, heavily loaded with conditionals. The conditionality of this utterance is then underlined with his final word, "possibility."

Misunderstanding speech acts often leads to an inaccurate and unacceptable intelligence analysis procedure (Shuy 1990). In this case, the prosecution did a very poor intelligence analysis.

TOPIC RECYCLING AND AMBIGUITY

Nevertheless, the two interviews with these clients were central to the government's case against Crow. The asymmetry of these interviews took several shapes. After the couple assured him that they had seen a doctor who told them that their problem persists, Crow then moved to the next step, preparing a contract for the doctor to release that information (step 4). While he was doing this, however, the clients recycled their previous topic, that they had seen a doctor nine times (step 2). Their topic recycling back to step 2 apparently constituted the clients' continuing effort to get Crow to say something inculpatory, although this idea apparently never entered his mind because he viewed them in the role they appeared to assume, that of unschooled but honest inner-city people. Their recyling this topic was too indirect for him to catch on to their trick. They did not unambiguously represent the illegality of their intentions and, of course, Crow had no clue that they were actually undercover agents. Over and over again, they asked Crow for directives about what they should do, always opening the door for some sort of nod and wink or directive that would suggest that they should do something illegal, which he didn't give them.

Another of the clients' recycled questions was, "Do you know of another doctor we should see?" Here they appeared to be fishing to see if Crow would name one of the doctors the government was already investigating. This effort failed, for his response was not helpful to them: "You can go to any doctor you want." If Crow was in cahoots with one of these questionable doctors, his language didn't reveal it.

Still another of their recycled questions was, "how many days should I do that work-miss-slip for?" Crow replied, "Did you miss a couple days?" Interestingly, the male agent answered, "okay," suggesting that he took Crow's reply as a directive. Crow may have been puzzled by this but he didn't bother to request clarification for there was nothing any more unusual about the agents' language here than in the rest of their inarticulate presentation, which included such sentences as "He is a medicine doctor" and "Yeah, they did a report cause he, either he told her upper back and neck and lower back or vice-versa." This was the kind of language Crow had to deal with. He tolerated their inarticulateness rather than taking the time to teach them, something that is not uncommon in the offices of professionals like doctors, lawyers, newspaper reporters, and even police interrogators. The paradox of such conversations is that two different understandings emerged. The agents probably thought Crow understood them and Crow probably thought they understood him, while neither actually did.

REFERENCING

At the heart of the government's charges against Crow was the following exchange:

Client: How many days should I, do that work, that miss work slip for that I got to get?

Crow: If you only went to the doctor, uh, when did you, when is he [your boss] going to say that you first went to the doctor?

Client: He's going to say like a couple days after that accident.

Crow: Okay. The day you went to the doctor, you probably missed that day and the next day.

Client: Okay.

Crow: So you find out from him [your boss] what the day is you went to the doctor.

Client: Okie-dokie.

This passage made it clear that since the agent seemed to be unable to recall what day he saw the doctor, Crow advised him to go to his boss and find out the day that he missed work, which is a logical date that he would have gone to see the doctor. But if we ignore the above bracketed part of this segment of their conversation that referenced who Crow meant by "him," it might seem unclear who the "him" refers to. The prosecution thought the "him" referred to the doctor and that Crow was telling the agent to go to one of the doctors who were already under suspicion. If true, this would indicate that Crow was a likely party to a fraudulent insurance claim and he was suborning perjury, even though his clear earlier advice was that his clients could go to *any* doctor they wanted. In truth, the doctor that the agent allegedly was seeing was one of the suspected physicians, but Crow had no way of knowing this since the suspected doctor's name had not been made public. The government's reading of Crow's last statement above would have to be: "So you find out from him [the doctor] what the day is you went to the doctor." This reading violates the way English speakers normally use prepositions to refer to immediate subjects. It is a clumsy, odd, and imperfect syntax that has no other support during the entire recordings of Crow's speech.

This was clear to the defense, and it was supported by linguistic analysis based on the structure of the speech event, the speech acts of directives, the grammatical scope of conditionals, and the ambiguity caused by the client's topic recycling. Misunderstanding or overlooking these language features often leads to inaccurate and unacceptable intelligence analysis procedures. In this case, the prosecution did a very poor intelligence analysis.

The trial ended well for Crow. In fact, it ended as soon as the prosecution rested, when Crow's defense attorney made the usual motion to dismiss the case, based on the fact that the government had failed to prove Crow's guilt. Much to the surprise of everyone present, the judge ruled in favor of Crow and the case was suddenly over. I understand that such rulings are rare and I felt privileged to be able to witness one in person. The only downside for me was that I didn't get the opportunity to testify about my analysis. But this was far outweighed by the encouragement this event gave me that judges can sometimes carry out their own effective intelligence analyses and come to just conclusions based on the evidence.

(12)
A United States senator's aborted perjury charge

There seem to be at least two common reasons for prosecutors to charge suspects with perjury. The first reason is the most obvious. People are charged with perjury when they make materially false statements under oath while trying to avoid responsibility or involvement in a criminal or civil matter, such as bribery, murder, or an illegal conspiracy. A second reason to charge people with perjury is when the prosecution fails to discover enough evidence to charge them with a more serious crime, such as corruption, and then resorts to charging them with a lesser crime, such as perjury. Of course, such a charge has to be based on comparable verifiable evidence that the person has indeed lied under oath.

To make a perjury charge stick, the prosecution has to be able to show that there is a conflict between what that person said and the provable facts that contrast with the person's testimony or other language evidence. The government may hold a strong belief that a person was lying, but belief alone isn't adequate. Equally ineffective proof of perjury comes from inferring the meaning of something that the person said. The first step taken by good prosecutors is to carry out an accurate intelligence analysis of the available evidence and to make a careful distinction between inference and known facts. Otherwise, their cases could go up in smoke during the trial.

In other books, I have described criminal cases in which the prosecutors have done less-than-sterling intelligence analyses, resulting in the expenditure of huge sums of public money, and then losing their cases when the evidence they believed was sufficiently incriminating ultimately failed to bring a conviction (Shuy 2005). In the *United States v. John DeLorean*, for example, the many covert tape-recordings of this car manufacturer with an agent showed clearly that the two men were referring to very different subjects when they finally both agreed, "investment is a good thing" (Shuy 1993). Linguistic analysis of the topic context in the entire sixty-three conversations that took place over many months made it clear that DeLorean continuously referenced investment to mean "someone making an investment in my company" while the agent tried to make it look like he meant "I agree to invest in your drug scheme." The prosecution, looking only at the last tape and ignoring everything that went before it, mistakenly thought they had finally caught DeLorean when he agreed, "investment is a good thing." Yes, he agreed, but not to what the prosecution thought. Had the prosecutors done a discourse analysis of all sixty-three conversations, they could have discovered this, but prosecutors don't usually do discourse analyses or examine the entire context of a series of conversations. Instead, they tend to look for individual, potentially incriminating features that, in isolation of the context, can look bad for the target. DeLorean's "investment is a good thing" is a classic example of this.

GOOD INTELLIGENCE ANALYSIS

Although this book examines several perjury cases in which prosecutors failed to do adequate intelligence analyses, this should be balanced with descriptions of cases in which effective intelligence analysis stopped a perjury prosecution from happening. One example of a district attorney's carefully done intelligence analysis of tape-recorded evidence related to the perjury investigation of the U.S. senator from Illinois, Roland Burris.

Burris was appointed to the U.S. Senate to replace the Illinois Senate seat of then-senator Barak Obama, who was elected president of the United States in November 2008. It is standard procedure in Illinois for the governor to have the authority to replace senators in such circumstances, but a serious problem with this procedure was that the current governor, Rod Blagojevich, had recently been arrested on federal corruption charges. Among other things, the governor was suspected to trying to sell the appointment to the vacated Senate seat to the highest bidder, or what the media called "pay for play." A month before the state legislature removed him from office, Blagojevich appointed Burris to Obama's vacant Senate seat, a decision that led some, including the media, to believe that Burris had been the highest cash bidder.

In January 2009, the state impeachment committee called Burris to testify as part of its investigation of Governor Blagojevich, during which testimony he denied that he had any contact with the governor or his representatives during the period before Blagojevich appointed him to that post. And then, three days after his testimony, Burris submitted an affidavit correcting his testimony, now saying that he had actually talked about his desire for this Senate appointment with Rob Blagojevich, the governor's brother, chief of staff, and campaign fund-raiser. This led some to believe that Burris had been trying to hide this discussion from the special committee and that he had possibly committed perjury when he at first denied that he had any contact with the governor or his staff.

At this point, the public sentiment against Burris was strong, for after all, previously he had associated closely with the allegedly corrupt governor Rod Blagojevich, and initially he had not been forthright with the impeachment committee about his past conversations with the governor's brother while openly promoting himself as the best replacement for the vacant Senate seat. Now came another challenge to his innocence when the FBI revealed that it had made covert tape-recordings in the governor's office, which included a conversation between Burris and the governor's brother, Rob Blagojevich.

For some time the FBI had been recording phone calls secretly to and from Blagojevich and his staff, including a seven-minute conversation between Blagojevich's brother Rob and Burris on November 13, 2008. On it, Burris spoke about how he couldn't help the governor by giving him a fund-raiser, how he would like to win the appointment to the vacant Senate seat, and how he would prefer not to run into trouble by giving anyone the impression that he might be trying to buy that Senate seat. Many, including the investigators, believed that Burris was engaging in crass negotiation during this call, or as it was referred to in the media, "pay to play." They also believed that Burris had lied by failing to mention this conversation when the impeachment committee interviewed him about his role, if any, in the governor's alleged corrupt activities. But belief by itself doesn't cut it. The prosecutor realized that he needed proof, and he wasn't sure that this phone call provided it.

In a perjury accusation, language is the major evidence. To this point, external circumstances made it look as though Burris might be guilty of the pay-to-play game. Any friend or associate of Governor Blagojevich during that time period was considered tainted, especially someone who admittedly had curried the governor's favor. Now add to this the fact that Burris's conversation had been recorded in the covert FBI operation and the public's general impression of him became very negative. To that point, there was no factual evidence that Burris had actually paid or promised to pay the governor to be appointed to the Senate seat, so the language evidence that Burris actually provided on that tape would be the deciding factor about whether he could be indicted for perjury. One question facing the prosecutor was whether the conversation contained damaging inferences, coded language, or other nods and winks that might indicate pay for play.

The prosecutor spent four months analyzing the taped conversation, Burris's statement under oath before the Illinois impeachment committee, and his affidavit in which he stated that he later remembered that he had that one conversation with Governor Blagojevich's brother. The prosecutor apparently did a careful intelligence analysis of this evidence without the help of linguistic advice and, based on what he found, he came to the same conclusions that a linguist might have made if the prosecutor had asked for such help. This leads to the question of what a linguistic analysis of the taped conversation might have told him. If the prosecutor had sought such help, a linguist likely would have come to the same conclusion, but probably quicker.

TOPIC ANALYSIS AS A CLUE TO INTENTIONS

The first thing that a discourse topic analysis would point out is one rather obvious clue to Burris's intent. He did not initiate that conversation; Rob Blagojevich did. One might expect venal and anxious persons seeking to buy an appointment to have initiated such a call themselves and bring up the topic as their major agenda item. A topic analysis of this conversation looks like this:

Topic	*Burris*	*Blagovetich*
1.	greeting	
2.		(small talk by both)
3.	I know you're gonna make me king	
4.	I wanna figure out what to do	

5.		we're trying to build a war chest
6.	I'm interested in replacing Obama	
7.	a fund-raiser would have negative connotations	
8.	Rod and I would catch hell	
9.	I could give a check myself	
10.	My law partner too	
11.		We've got a number of events scheduled
12.	Maybe I could join one	
13.		We have no law firms supporting us
14	I hope for consideration for the appointment	
15.	I'd handle the press	
16.		Do what you think is fair
17.		If I can think where to fit you guys in
18.	no conflicts for either of us	
19.		How's your business?
20.		Write the checks and we'll try to tie you in
21.	I'll do something by December 15	

22.		(pre-closing)
23.	Keep me in mind	
24.		(closing)

Topics that are introduced by speakers are one of the best indications of their conversational agenda. Of the twenty-four topics, four are the formulaic non-substantive topics of greeting, small talk, pre-closing, and closing, which are common features in most conversations. Of the remaining twenty substantive topics, Burris introduced fourteen of them and Blagojevich introduced only six. Frequently, when persons introduce the most topics, in this case at a ratio of more than two to one, it suggests that they are the more powerful communicators and control the conversation. But this is not always true, especially when one speaker is so persistent in presenting his agenda. It's also true in this call that both speakers were in some ways superordinates, Blagojevich being the conduit to his brother, the governor, and Burris being a potentially heavy donor to the governor's campaign for reelection. And they were also virtually equal as subordinates, with Blagojevich needing Burris's support and Burris needing Blagojevich's favor. Since their conversational power was about equal, it is important to examine their conversational agendas, as revealed by their recycled topics.

Burris's topics are:

1. He wants to be appointed to the senate seat: topics 3, 4, 6, 14, 15, and 22.
2. He has problems with personally sponsoring a fund-raiser: topics 7, 8, 18, and 21.
3. He is willing to make personal campaign contribution: topics 9, 10, 12, and 20.

Blagojevich has only one topic, which recycled his agenda five times:

1. He wants Burris to sponsor a fund-raiser: topics 5, 11, 13, 16, 17, and 19.

Six of Burris's topics proactively expressed his desire for the Senate seat while his other eight topics were reactive to Blagojevich's five recycled topics of wanting Burris to hold a fund-raiser for a future campaign.

Comparing only the number of topics introduced by each speaker, it is clear that Burris dominates the conversation, introducing fourteen of the substantive topics to Rob Blagojevich's six. But it is also clear that even though the governor's brother initiated the phone call, Burris tried to take over the caller's topic and convert it to his own agenda. Burris introduced topics relevant to (but not supportive of) Blagojevich's agenda of getting Burris to hold a fund-raiser, repeatedly explaining his problems with his holding a fund-raiser, and he introduced his alternative topic of making a personal contribution to the campaign. But he spread his own agenda of wishing to be appointed to the Senate seat throughout the entire conversation, another indication of his undeniably strong agenda. It is also clear that none of Rob Blagojevich's topics were related Burris's main topic of securing the Senate-seat appointment. In fact, his only response to Burris's first mention of wanting this appointment was "you and a million others," suggesting strongly that appointment to the seat was even far from Rob Blagojevich's own interest or agenda in this call.

Next, we turn to the actual words and expression used by the two men in the crucial topics. After Burris answered the phone and the two men engaged in the usual small talk, the governor's brother introduced the main point of his call:

> Blagojevich: We've had a number of conversations about, you know, anything you might be able to do . . . here before the end of

> the year for Rod. Again, we're trying to get as much as we can in his war chest, so that when he has to, you know, disclose in January.

We see from this that the governor's brother introduced the topic that his job required him to do—to try to raise funds for the governor's reelection. This might have been a subtle ploy to get Burris to offer to buy the Senate seat, but his actual words did not support this hypothesis as the conversation continued:

Burris:	Yeah, right... and now... answer me this question because I'm very interested in trying to replace Obama.
Blagojevich:	You and a million other people.

Burris then changed the topic and forthrightly stated his interest in getting the governor to appoint him to Obama's vacated Senate seat. Whether or not such self-promotion is appropriate, it is not a criminal matter. Blagojevich's sarcastic answer strongly suggests that Burris's appointment certainly was not on his agenda. Next, Burris realized that if he did any serious fund-raising, it could look like he was trying to buy the appointment to replace Obama:

> Burris: So if I put on a fund-raiser now... it has so many negative connotations that Burris is trying to buy an appointment from the governor for the senate seat... I've been just holding off calling you... I'm trying to figure out how to deal with this and still be in the consideration for the appointment... then Rod and I both gonna catch hell. And if I do get appointed that means I bought it... My people who I'm trying to raise money from are gonna look at me, "yeah what's that all

> about, Roland?"... I'm in a dilemma right now, wanting to help the governor... I know I could give him a check myself. I didn't know how to deal with this situation.

Burris doesn't want to "catch hell" by holding a fund-raiser that may look like toadying up to the governor, and he also doesn't want the governor to be criticized for appointing him to the Senate in exchange for Burris's political favor of raising money for him. As Burris put it, it was a "dilemma." A venal way to do this would be for Burris to produce a quid pro quo here, indicating something like, "Sure I'll raise money for him if he appoints me Senator." But Burris didn't say this, or even hint at it. In fact, he said he couldn't do it because it would look like he was doing it as a quid pro quo. He was willing to help the governor by giving him his own personal check, but he couldn't do a big fund-raiser without bringing suspicion on him for his motives. The governor's brother agreed, without even soliciting something that could be useful as the basis of an indictment. He responded without connecting Burris's offer with a promise of appointment to the Senate:

> Blagojevich: I'll stand by. I mean if you wanna write a check and have Fred [Burris's law partner] write a check or have someone else write a check that'd be great.

It's possible that Rob Blagojevich was hinting that "write a check" could be for buying the appointment, but the overall discourse context argues against such an interpretation. Burris had talked only about writing a personal check for the governor's campaign, not about a check to buy the Senate seat. In fact, Burris had explained that by not holding a fund-raiser, he would avoid such an accusation. In any case, when the governor's brother said that Fred could write a check and someone else could write a check, it would take a stretch of the imagination to understand this to be hinting that these other people would be writing checks that would help Burris buy the appointment.

The rest of the conversation concerned Burris's topic about his consulting firm that is in financial trouble, until the end, when Rob Blagojevich repeated his conversational agenda:

Blagojevich:	Please keep me in mind and you know if you guys can just write checks, that'd be fine, if we can find a way for you to tie in.
Burris:	Okay, okay. Well...I will personally do something, okay.
Blagojevich:	Hey, you're a good friend. I'll pass on your message.
Burris:	Please do, and tell Rod to keep me in mind for that seat, would ya?
Blagojevich:	I'll let him know.

Here we see the two men exchanging their competing major topics once more. Blagojevich made another pitch for contributions but by now appeared to have given up on the idea of Burris organizing a fund-raiser, while Burris stayed with his promise of a personal campaign contribution ("I will personally do something") and asked that the governor's brother tell the governor to keep him in mind for the seat. One might hypothesize that this is code for I'll pay for play, but the context of the entire conversation does not support this notion. Blagojevich's final, "I'll let him know" is blandly unpromising.

INFERENCES AND POSSIBLE DECEPTION

Perhaps Blagojevich's "If we can find a way to tie you in" might have raised the prosecutor's eyebrows, because it could have at least two possible meanings: (1) tie Burris into the governor's campaign, which would indicate that Burris would endorse the governor by connecting his name to the fund-raising effort; or (2) tie Burris in by putting him at the top of the list of potential appointees to the senate seat. Again, the predominating themes and agendas of the conversation suggest strongly that this meant including and connecting Burris with the fund-raising campaign.

The prosecutor probably also explored the possibility of inferred meaning when Blagojevich said:

> Blagojevich: We've had a number of conversations about, you know, anything you might be able to do.

This suggests strongly that he and Burris have talked before about campaign contributions for the governor. If these conversations occurred, they were apparently not tape-recorded so there was nothing the prosecutor could do about using them. In any case, although the governor's brother didn't say or even hint that these conversations were about a quid pro quo for the Senate seat, it was clear that they had talked about Burris helping with the governor's war chest at some time in the past. The prosecutor apparently felt that talking about fund-raising in either the past or present was not equivalent a quid pro quo for buying this Senate seat. Furthermore, the fact that Burris had omitted any mention of this conversation in his testimony before the impeachment committee would be a difficult point on which to hang a perjury charge, because it is natural and obvious for campaigners to talk with their friends about such matters. And it would be very possible for Burris to have forgotten about one such incident.

The following statement by the governor's brother might also have been a candidate for inferred meaning:

> Blagojevich: "We're trying to get as much as we can in his war chest"

This could be understood to mean either: (1) "we want you to pay us for appointing you," or (2) "we want you to contribute to our campaign." The prosecutor apparently decided on the second meaning, and he was quite right to do so, because the discourse in the rest of the conversation focuses on Burris giving a personal check to the campaign, while at the same time explaining how it might look as though he was trying to buy the Senate seat if he organized a fund-raiser for the governor. In this, Burris seemed to be following the advice of St. Paul, who said, "avoid the very appearance of evil." (1 Thessalonians 5:22)

Finally, the prosecutor may have explored the possible inference in the following:

> Burris: Please do, and tell Rod to keep me in mind for that seat.

"Keep me in mind" is a far cry from "tell me how much I need to pay to buy the Senate seat." The prosecutor must have understood this referential meaning and decided that Burris was not offering to buy the seat. Even if he was hinting at this, the prosecutor would have a difficult time convincing a jury that specific X really means inferred Y.

The public suspicion that Burris was tying to pay for his appointment to the United States Senate did not influence this prosecutor to try to bend the vague statements by both men to make them appear to be venal. For this he should be congratulated, for he did a fair and proper intelligence analysis of the conversation, and, although it took four months of work, he came to the best conclusion, based on the only tangible evidence available, and he did so without the benefit of linguistic analysis. His comments about his decision not to indict Burris for perjury were reported in the press:

> In a written statement issued on Friday, Mr. Schmidt said that some of Mr. Burris's statements in January before a committee of

> state lawmakers (who were at the time considering whether to impeach Mr. Blagojevich) had been "vague," but said: "vague statements cannot support a perjury charge. A review of the evidence, consisting of numerous interviews and documents, indicates that there is insufficient evidence to prove Senator Burris made a statement that he knew to be false," Mr. Schmidt said. (*New York Times*, June 20, 2009)

A few months later, the U.S. Senate Select Committee on Ethics also reviewed this case and on November 20, 2009, the Committee sent Senator Burris a Public Letter of Qualified Admonition, saying that this admonition was based on "actions and statements reflecting unfavorably upon the Senate in connection with your appointment and seating in the Senate." It further said that when Burris testified before the impeachment committee, he "should have known" that he was providing incorrect, inconsistent, misleading, or incomplete information to the public, the Senate, and those conducting legitimate inquiries, and that his short phone call with the governor's brother, discussed above, "while not rising to the level of an explicit *quid pro quo,* was inappropriate." The committee further complained: "it was not until your second affidavit... that you disclosed additional contacts with associates of the Governor."

So what was the basis of this admonition? Apparently it was that Burris "should have known" about the conversation he said he didn't remember when he testified before the governor's impeachment committee. The ethics committee falls short of saying that Burris should have remembered this, but that is the most likely interpretation possible here. The committee simply didn't believe Burris' lack of memory, even scoffing a bit, saying: "It was not until your second affidavit and subsequent press statements that you disclosed additional contacts with the associates of the Governor." Here the committee's use of the plural forms in "contacts" and "associates" is curiously exaggerated, since the evidence in question shows only one contact and only one associate.

In the context of recovered memory, the word, "disclosed," also suggests that Burris was hiding something. With only their inferences that he was lying, and with the prosecutor's unwillingness to indict him, the ethics committee faced a serious problem. They couldn't impeach him on the basis of inferences or for being investigated and found legally blameless. What seemed to matter most was that he couldn't remember what he "should have known," and that he actually asked the brother of the indicted (but not yet tried) governor to put in a good word for him to be appointed to the Senate along with his promise to contribute to governor's reelection campaign. Apparently, it didn't matter that Burris did not initiate this call. The ethics committee's letter to Burris concluded that they found that his actions and statements reflected unfavorably on the Senate. Apparently, this means that answering the phone call from the governor's brother was enough to cause Burris's admonishment. If it means that prospective candidates cannot request being considered for appointment to a Senate seat, many politicians should be equally admonished. In short, the ethics committee appeared to be covering its ethical tail with a rather transparently couched sense of righteousness.

Although the prosecutor's decision not to indict Senator Burris did not benefit from the assistance of a linguist, this is not to say that such help is never needed. Linguistics provides the analytical tools, procedures, and even concepts that can be used to specify and explain decisions that, like this one, were otherwise made with good sense and intuition. And they can do this quickly and scientifically. It is fortunate that this prosecutor was able to analyze the evidence more competently and effectively than the U.S. Senate Select Committee on Ethics could seem to manage.

(13)
A priest's aborted perjury charge

In early December 2007, Father Joseph Sica was indicted for perjury for what he said in his testimony a year earlier before a Dauphin County, Pennsylvania grand jury. The prosecutor had called Father Sica as a witness in an ongoing investigation of Louis DeNaples, a Scranton businessman who owned the Mount Airy Resort in the Pocono Mountains area. The government suspected that DeNaples had close ties with the late Russell Bufalino, who had served lengthy prison sentences in the 1970s and 1980s on charges of murder and racketeering. At the same time, DeNaples was also separately indicted for perjury for allegedly lying about his relationship with Bufalino's associate, William D'Elia, who at that time allegedly headed the Bufalino crime family. The prosecutor's admitted goal was to remove DeNaples from the gaming industry. Toward that end, Father Sica was called to testify about his current relationship with DeNaples and his own past relationship with Bufalino.

The prosecutor believed that during his testimony Father Sica lied to protect his good friend, DeNaples. There was no question about their friendship, for in his grand jury testimony, Sica mentioned over and over again how they grew up in the same neighborhood, often visited and dined with each other, and were very close friends. Based on some facts (notes and photos) that the prosecutor discovered, he thought his intelligence analysis leading to Sica's indictment was relatively strong, but to prove perjury he needed to back up his factual intelligence with Father Sica's actual language that he used at the grand jury hearing. But even the factual evidence that the prosecutor gathered turned out to lack contextual information that later became clear. In brief, the prosecutor inferred things from the intelligence gathering that later proved it to be faulty.

The prosecution of Father Sica was not popular among central Pennsylvanians. He held advanced degrees in philosophy and theology and had written a spiritual-guidance book and many articles in Catholic newspapers across the country. His Christian service deeply impressed his community, including his creative programs for the poor and homeless and his successful efforts to provide transportation, meals, home repairs, and other services to the Scranton area's neediest populations. At the time he was indicted, he was serving as chaplain in a local hospital, having recently returned to the same Christian service that he performed when he was ordained some twenty-five years earlier.

The prosecutor claimed he was interested in Father Sica only to the extent he could reveal something incriminating about DeNaples' connection with Bufalino and D'Elia, who were thought to have a criminal influence related to DeNaples' casino in the Pocono Mountains. He did his homework before making his decision to indict, collecting information that would seem to associate Sica closely with both DeNaples and Bufalino. His intelligence gathering included photos of Father Sica with Bufalino that were taken at his confirmation ceremony as priest, an undated thank-you note that he sent to Mr. and Mrs. Bufalino, and a tape-recorded interview of him on a local radio station after his indictment. The prosecutor believed that this factual evidence would clearly show that in the past Father Sica had a close personal relationship with Bufalino. If the priest indeed had such a relationship, the prosecution could likely get useful information from him.

Therefore, when Father Sica testified to the grand jury that he had no personal relationship with Bufalino, the prosecutor believed he had enough language evidence to charge him with perjury.

The grand jury indicted Father Sica on December 27, 2007, and he was arrested on January 2, 2008. Although the prosecutor believed he had a strong case, his superior, the district attorney, wasn't as impressed, because his own intelligence analysis of the evidence led him suspect that the perjury charge might not be likely to succeed at trial. To avoid a possible failed prosecution, the district attorney asked Rob Leonard and me to do an analysis of the language used during the priest's grand jury appearance. We agreed to do the analysis together, as we often do. However, this was the first time that we had ever been asked by a district attorney to provide an analysis outside the context of an actual trial. As such, it meant that linguistics became part of the intelligence analysis, of which I will say more in chapter 14.

THE PROSECUTOR'S UNDEFINED USE OF "CLOSE PERSONAL RELATIONSHIP"

The central issue in this case hinged on the meaning and mutual understanding of the phrase, "personal relationship" and the modified phrase, "close personal relationship." References to types of human communicative interaction vary in degree with such expressions as "seeing," "meeting," "contacting," "having a relationship with," "knowing well," and "personal relationship." Descriptive modifiers can help define these by prefacing them with qualitative descriptors such as "intimate," "very close," "close," "frequent," "regular," "casual," "intermittent," or "distant."

The speech-event context in which the expression "close personal relationship" was used is always important. This context was a grand jury interrogation, in which answers to questions are required to be truthful, clear, and precise. The questions have that same requirement, as noted throughout this book, because it is critically important that persons suspected of a crime be able to determine the intended meaning of the questions put to them.

The indictment cited various exchanges in the grand jury testimony about Father Sica's "personal relationship" and "close personal relationship" with Buffalino:

Q: How many times did you meet Russell Bufalino?
A: At the present time I really can't recall.
Q: When was the last time that you recall having any contact with Russell Bufalino?
A: Twenty some years ago.
Q: You wouldn't, it was just a, you met him?
A: Yes, sir.
Q: There, you didn't have any sort of personal relationship with Russell Bufalino?
A: No. When I was a deacon in Sayre, do you want me to tell you how I met him?
Q: Sure.

Father Sica was uncertain about what the prosecutor meant by "personal relationship," so after pausing to think about it, he requested clarification by suggesting that the question must have meant how he *met* Bufalino. He then volunteered at length how he had met the man some two decades earlier when he was serving as chaplain in a hospital and when Bufalino and his wife came to visit a patient there. Not satisfied with the priest's definition, the prosecutor continued to probe:

Q: Did you have any personal relationship beyond that with Mr. and Mrs. Bufalino?
A: No.
Q: It was just a chance meeting?
A: Yes.

The prosecutor then pursued the matter further:

Q: Certainly you didn't have any personal relationship with Russell Bufalino?
A: No.
Q: Or any member of his family?
A: I met his wife, Carrie... the same way, at the hospital...
Q: Did you have any personal relationship beyond that with Mr. and Mrs. Russell Bufalino?
A: No.

The prosecutor then introduced the factual intelligence that he had gathered: a photo of Father Sica in the company of Russell Bufalino and another photo of him with D'Elia, Bufalino and others. Both photos appeared to have been taken at some kind of party or celebration. The prosecutor also introduced a note written by Father Sica to Bufalino beginning "Dear Russ," telling him that he had written to the governor as Bufalino's character witness and another thank-you note from Father Sica to the Bufalinos.

Finally, the prosecutor confronted Father Sica with a tape-recorded interview that he gave to a local radio station shortly after he was indicted, in which he said that sometimes, when he would go home to visit his parents, Bufalino, who lived in the same community, would invite him to dinner. He added that Bufalino gave him a gift of $100 at his ordination service some twenty-five years ago, for which Father Sica wrote a thank-you note on the back of a photo, and that Mrs. Bufalino at one time had asked him to give her husband a "blessing and prayer" before he was sent to prison in the 1980s.

The indictment concluded: "The evidence demonstrates clearly that Sica had a substantial relationship with Russell Bufalino. The testimony to the contrary is false."

This intelligence information constituted all of the factual evidence that the prosecutor had gathered in his effort to convict Father Sica of perjury. His reasoning was that these facts defined a close personal relationship, regardless of the fact that they took place at some time in the distant past and regardless of whether they were related to the common parish life and work of a priest.

FATHER SICA'S IMPLICIT DEFINITION OF A "CLOSE PERSONAL RELATIONSHIP"

Proof that Father Sica had lied in his testimony depended heavily on a meeting of their minds about what "a close personal relationship" meant. Whenever there is confusion about the meaning of words, participants in an exchange have the opportunity to request clarification. Five times the prosecutor asked Father Sica if he had a personal relationship with Bufalino, to which the priest answered that he did not. Next, the prosecutor upped the definition a bit, adding the modifier, "close," and asking, "Did you have a *close* personal relationship with Russell Bufalino?" Father Sica answered, "not close." After a brief pause, Father Sica revised his answer slightly to "not close and personal."

Like the prosecutor, Father Sica did not offer an explicit verbal definition of "a personal relationship" or "a close personal relationship." But just as the prosecutor had used photos, a thank-you note, and radio interview to provide his implicit meaning of the expression, earlier in his same testimony Father Sica had provided his own implicit meaning of a "close personal relationship" as he testified about his relationship with Louis DeNaples:

Q: Do you know a fellow by the name of Louis A. DeNaples?
A: Extremely well.

Q: How long have you known him?

A: Fifty years, my whole life. [He] had his junkyard, where his mom and dad raised all the kids. And so we were kids, we would go down there... we would play... and so that's how I got to know him. He and my dad were very close... So we just kind of knew Mr. and Mrs. DeNaples as our family... And then when my mother and father both died, I became much closer to Louis and Betty and to all of his children... If I would be home only on weekends I would stop over to see him or he'd be at my dad's house.

Q: How frequent was your contact with Louis DeNaples in 1992?

A: I would say consistent and constant contact with him.

Q: It would be common to share meals with him?

A: Most definitely... Frequently and consistently... Like last night I was there.

Q: Is it fair to say that in the last ten years and longer you have been virtually a member of the DeNaples family?

A: Yes, but I consider myself a close friend.

Here Father Sica provided his own implicit definition of what it means to be a close personal friend. He didn't give a dictionary definition, but his examples are compellingly clear.

SOCIAL CONTEXT ISSUES

The prosecutor's focus on the photos in evidence did not consider the social fact that at ceremonial events such as ordinations, it is common practice for group photos to be taken as mementos of such events. His focus also failed to consider that it is commonplace to give gifts to the person being honored, and it is equally commonplace for the honoree to follow conventional politeness rules by writing thank-you notes to the persons who gave the gifts, including gifts of money. That Father Sica would irregularly and infrequently accept an invitation to dine with the Bufalinos when he traveled to his home area to visit his parents indicates that this too was a polite (or possibly priestly) gesture, but it falls short of suggesting anything like the intimacy defined by his close relationship with the DeNaples family, noted above. His trip to the Bufalino home to offer prayers and a blessing to an acquaintance who requested a visit from a priest falls into the category of Father Sica's professional obligation rather than as a social visit.

MEMORY ISSUES

After the prosecutor learned of the radio interview in which Father Sica said that he had received a $100 gift from Bufalino at his ordination ceremony some twenty-five years earlier, he amended his original complaint, thinking he was strengthening it, noting that Father Sica would sometimes visit the Bufalinos when he went home to visit his parents, and that he prayed for and blessed Bufalino (who died in 1994) before he was sent off to prison. The prosecutor suspected that Father Sica didn't report any of this during his testimony before the grand jury because he was trying to protect his close friend, DeNaples. But since the prosecutor's stated purpose for calling Father Sica before the grand jury was to obtain information that would show that DeNaples had a close relationship with the alleged crime family head, William D'Elia, his effort was clearly unsuccessful. Father Sica testified that he had no memory of ever socializing with D'Elia or talking with DeNaples about him.

After failures like this, the next step in many criminal investigations is to charge witnesses with perjury if you can't find anything else to charge. But since in his grand jury testimony Father Sica clearly said that he didn't recall the distant events of the gift, dinners with the Bufalinos, and the event when he prayed and blessed Bufalino, but then recalled these later on the radio interview, the prosecutor thought the priest was lying about his alleged memory loss.

The first thing to keep in mind is that Father Sica was trying to recall events that had happened many years ago. The details of his ordination twenty-five years earlier could easily fade. Many photos were taken. Many gifts were given. Many thank-you notes were written. Now, in his grand jury testimony, the prosecutor asked Father Sica to remember things that were blurry in his memory. Yes, he could say "I don't recall," and this is the answer he gave to many questions, including:

- how many times he had met with Bufalino;
- whether Bufalino was at his ordination ceremony;
- whether he [DeNaples] ever socialized with D'Elia;
- whether he [Sica] attended the 1983 Italian American Civil Rights dinner;
- whether DeNapes attended the 1983 Italian American Civil Rights dinner;
- how he met Dave Ostico;
- whether he ever saw D'Elia at DeNaples' office;
- whether he ever heard DeNaples speak of D'Elia; and
- whether he ever heard DeNaples speak of Bufalino.

There is no way to get into the mind and memory of people, especially people who are in a grand jury speech event in which exact memory is called for. Attorneys regularly advise witnesses to say that they don't remember rather to give partial information, estimates, or guesses.

Further complicating a charge of perjury is the fact that Father Sica's responses to the crucial factual evidence were: "I have no *present* recollection of that." Recollection comes and goes. He later managed to recollect some things in the radio interview that he couldn't recollect at the time he took his pressure-filled seat on the witness stand. In any case, as Garner's *Dictionary of Modern Legal Usage* (1995) points out, "to recollect is to find something stored further back in the mind, while to remember is to recall what is ready at hand in one's memory." This definition applied to Father Sica. The things the prosecutor asked about were stored back in his mind, not ready at hand.

THE CHARGES WERE DROPPED

After the district attorney received our analysis of the contrasting definitions of "close personal relationship," the role of social context, and the vagaries of recovered memory, he recognized that the prosecutor's indictment was seriously flawed. He subsequently dropped the perjury charges against Father Sica on April 14, 2009, saying:

> Perjury cases are very difficult in that the language is the weapon we need to prove. We engaged expert linguists, something a little different but it is a perjury case, where the precision of questioning is important.

Perhaps the time has finally come for prosecutors to call on linguists to discover that the way language is used in perjury cases is central to their intelligence analysis.

(14)
The advantages and dangers of intelligence analysis in perjury cases

Many people who are charged with perjury deserve it, while some others do not. I'm not trying to make a case for everyone's innocence, because there are many liars who try to fool the government. Nor am I saying that the government is usually wrong when they indict someone for perjury. The question always boils down to whether the intelligence information was gathered properly and whether that intelligence was properly analyzed. This chapter briefly reviews the way intelligence was gathered and analyzed in these cases, then summarizes the linguistic tools that were applied.

ADVANTAGES OF GOOD INTELLIGENCE ANALYSIS

Chapters 12 and 13, describing the cases of Roland Burris and Father Joseph Sica, show how the prosecutors did a very good job of assessing the rather weak intelligence gathered for them. Their intelligence analysis prevented the government from possibly being embarrassed for losing these cases but, more important, it avoided the anguish these two men would have had to endure during and after the their trials. In the case of Donald Crow (chapter 11), it was the judge who did the intelligence analysis that stopped the trial process after it had begun. These three decisions not to proceed saved the government precious time and resources, and those three intelligence analysts should be congratulated for their perceptive work.

DANGERS OF POOR INTELLIGENCE ANALYSIS

Some serious questions remain, however, about the government's perjury charges in other cases described here. In some cases, the intelligence gathering was at fault. In other cases the problem was the intelligence analysis. And in some both were at fault.

The charge of perjury in the Bolles case in chapter 3 was highly questionable, and if the prosecutor had seriously considered the factors described in that chapter, he might have reconsidered his decision to indict. As noted, part of the problem was the confusing 6B Form that he had to complete in his bankruptcy application, and an equal part of the problem came from the prosecutor's own intelligence analysis.

The shipping company officials in chapters 7 and 8, among others, had schemas about the grand jury speech event that appeared to be effectively and unfairly used against them by their prosecutors, whose apparent need to win these cases may have overridden any effective intelligence analyses that they could have conducted.

The same can be said for the perjury charges against the Filipino-American doctor in chapter 9, whose case illustrates problems with both intelligence gathering by investigators and intelligence analysis by the prosecutor, who was apparently thrown off by his inability to understand cross-cultural and language-interference issues. In chapter 10, the prosecution of the Hawaiian Creole–speaking union representative, Steven Suyat, displayed the prosecutor's apparent need to win a case instead of first making an adequate intelligence analysis.

The subornation of perjury charge against lawyer Donald Crow in chapter 11 suffered from very questionable intelligence gathering, leading the judge to dismiss the charges after the prosecution tried to base its case on the tapes made by the undercover postal inspectors. In dismissing the case, the judge ruled that the prosecution's evidence had failed to show that Crow had acted illegally. In my years of experience, summary judgment rulings have happened very rarely. This judge should be lauded, however, for recognizing the weaknesses of both the intelligence gathering and the prosecutor's intelligence analysis.

More effective intelligence analysis likely would have prevented these cases from being brought in the first place, as it did the case of Senator Burris (chapter 12). The fact that the jury convicted some of these men, in spite of the linguistic evidence that indicated otherwise, is not a tribute to intelligence analysis done by the prosecutors. But they usually won anyway, which sadly may have been their primary motives.

POSSIBLE MOTIVATIONS FOR INDICTMENTS

Even more lingering doubts concern the government's motivation to charge these people in the first place. Bolles was clearly confused by the 6B Form he filled out when he declared bankruptcy. The ensuing hearing made it clear that he was confused about the meaning of terms in the form. By the end of his hearing, even the officials who questioned him could see this, because everything material appeared to have been clarified.

The perjury charges against Suyat, Dowd, Reilly, and the Filipino doctor may have been motivated by a desperate need to place the blame on someone for the bad acts that someone had done, whether or not they had the right "someone." Often the public rightfully has strong feelings against doctors who misdiagnose children, against illegal union picketers, and against someone who illegally dumped eleven thousand tons of incinerator ash in the ocean. Such public sentiments possibly may have swayed the prosecutors' decision-making processes in these cases. But who can know for sure? The prosecutors in these cases may have had sincere and honest motives that were, unfortunately, not swayed by linguistic analyses. And it's always possible that the linguistic analysis may not have been presented as effectively as it could have been.

On the other hand, one can begin to understand the prosecutors' motivations for charging Frank Serafini (chapter 4), because the different meanings of "reimbursed" also had escaped the attention of other judges in past cases. At least the judge in Serafini's case had precedent to guide him. But it is also suspected that some prosecutors may take a degree of delight in prosecuting public officials.

The case of Larry Kopp (chapter 5) was complicated by the fact that he was clearly guilty of helping to perpetuate a fraud, but it was considerably less clear that the government's tape-recorded evidence proved that he had committed perjury. When a person is guilty of one of the charged crimes, it's naturally tempting (but certainly not always the case) to feel that a jury might want to convict on all of the counts, perhaps believing that if a defendant is guilty of one thing, he's very likely guilty of the others as well.

Lawyer Donald Crow (chapter 11) suffered from falling into law enforcement's broad, somewhat random search for possible fraud and subornation of perjury. Law enforcement was trolling for illegality and had no particular reason to single him out other than the fact that his storefront law practice catered to a poorer class of citizens, where suborning perjury might be likely to occur. He was ripe for the picking. The investigators relied on a type of profiling, only in this investigation the usual sense of racial profiling worked in the opposite way than it usually does. The motivation to charge the attorney was not personal. He was sought out only because he belonged to a class of people that included lawyers and doctors working with a particular social class. One could hope that the search for illegal behavior, even that of suborning perjury, might begin with a hypothesis of individual guilt rather than one of potential class behavior.

(15) Some recommendations for analyzing perjury cases

Perjury, like most law cases, is largely about the use of language in the legal context. Based on my experience in hundreds of civil and criminal law suits, including dozens of perjury cases, it would appear that both prosecutors and defense lawyers could profit by learning more about the way language works as they carry out their own intelligence analyses. Most of the defense lawyers and prosecutors that I've worked with are tempted to become overly concerned about the smaller units of language, those individual words and sentences that seem to be important to their cases. For them, the important evidence is often found in single words, phrases, or sentences that stand out like smoking guns and that seem to be strong evidence of either guilt or innocence.

It is not surprising that people notice the smaller units of language first, because most people think about language as a construction of its smallest units, often its sounds, words, and sentences, rather its structure of whole discourse. We have to admit that even the historical development of linguistic science proceeded in the direction of smaller to larger language units. After many years of focusing on the sounds, morphemes, and syntax of language, only within the past few decades have linguists have been addressing the larger structures of discourse, speech acts, pragmatic meaning, and conversational strategies, all of which contextualize and cast important light on the smaller language units.

When we consider the entire context in which spoken and written language exists, we can view communicative meaning, intentions, and effectiveness in a way that is somewhat uncommon to most people, including some lawyers. Of course, communicative meaning exists on all levels of language, but the main task of listeners and readers is to try to understand the whole meaning of what is said or written as they think about the smaller parts that make it up. In the same way, the focus on larger communicative intent can also lead listeners and readers to overlook some of the critical smaller units of language. Both types of language are important, but it's easy to overlook meaning that becomes identifiable from the context in which language is used.

An example from the field of teaching children to read may illustrate this point. The ultimate goal of reading a text is to capture its essential meaning, not to sound out every letter-sound correspondence. It is problematic when a child does a great job of sounding out the letters while missing the overall meaning of the text. This is not to say that the smaller units, the letters and words, are unimportant, but rather that they themselves are not the essential meaning. Children become competent readers when they understand the meaning of the overall discourse.

My point here is that the procedure for an effective intelligence analysis should be turned on its head to proceed from the larger language units to the smaller ones. The analyst should first focus on aspects of the speech event in which the participants communicate, on their schemas and assumptions about the topics introduced, on their agendas, on the felicity of their speech acts, and on their ability and willingness to be conversationally cooperative. The smaller language units, such as the words and sentences, are embedded in this overall intention to understand meaning and their significance to the case must be seen in relationship to the larger units of the discourse.

This means that intelligence analysts should examine the language evidence in their law cases more or less in the following order, beginning with the larger language units and only finally going to the smaller ones:

1. What do the participants consider the *speech event* to be?
2. What are the participants' *schemas?*
3. What are the participants' *agendas as revealed by their topics*?
4. How do the participants' *responses* relate to the questions asked?
5. How do the participants apply the *cooperative principle*?
6. What *speech acts* do the participants use or not use? Are they used felicitously?
7. What *conversational strategies* do the participants use?
8. Is the *recency principle* at work?
9. What *ambiguities* exist and how are they resolved, if at all?
10. Which words and phrases are *semantically significant* to the case?

Based on my experience in both civil and criminal law cases, many lawyers seem to focus primarily, and sometimes exclusively, on step 10. Each case is different, of course, and not all of these ten analytical procedures will be relevant to every case. But proceeding from larger language units to the smaller ones is important, because the smaller items, such as the words, are often more clearly understood in relation to such things as the speech event, schemas, and agendas.

Whether lawyers do this themselves or ask for linguistic help, the following recommendations can lead to more effective intelligence analyses:

1. Identify the speech event

The first way to view a case is to consider the communicative expectations of the speech event of the participatory situation (Gumperz 1990, 8–11). In most perjury cases, the speech event is the courtroom interaction. Lawyers participate in this speech event regularly and they are very familiar with it. But does their understanding always match what does witnesses think it is? Steven Suyat (chapter 10) had a very different impression of how he was expected to respond to the prosecutor's questions in the grand jury speech event. When the prosecutor asked him, "What does the word 'scab' mean?" Suyat felt that since this was a very formal and unfamiliar event, he was being asked to give a formal dictionary definition, not his own sense of the word. He knew that the prosecutor controlled the questions and was totally in charge. He knew that he was just a relatively uneducated carpenter who couldn't possibly meet the requirement that he thought the speech event required him to accomplish. And besides, since the prosecutor didn't ask him what he personally thought the word meant, he had to make his own decision about how to answer.

In the speech event of Crow's interview with his client (chapter 11), this lawyer followed the standard lawyer-client interview speech event routines and procedures despite the difficulties he faced with a client who continuously feigned ignorance. It wasn't Crow who violated the standards of this speech event; it was the undercover client who threw the exchange into a muddle, leading to Crow being accused of not following standard procedure.

The nature of the speech event should also cause lawyers to consider any extra-linguistic aspects that are involved. In the case of Bolles (chapter 3), the participants at his bankruptcy hearing apparently overlooked or ignored many extra-linguistic clues about Bolles's ineptness as a businessman, his many misunderstandings of the meanings of important words they were using, and his disfluencies as a speaker, leading to his indictment for perjury.

Some may think it something of a stretch to consider that a speech event can extend to written discourse, but the license application forms that a prospective hunter has to fill out and sign can have a similar effect on a reader. The implied and unstated meanings of the Montana hunting license application confused and stymied not only Dr. Turpin (chapter 6) but, fortunately for him, they also confused and irritated the Montana jurors who brought a not-guilty verdict in Turpin's trail.

2. Identify the schemas of the participants

We have all found ourselves in one of those "trains passing in the night" situations when we thought we had a clear understanding of the topic while our conversational partner had a quite different one. Even within the same speech event, such as a grand jury interview, the participants can find themselves on different wavelengths of understanding.

For example, shipping executive Reilly (chapter 8) assumed that his role was to report only known and verifiable facts, not guesses or suppositions, and yet he was convicted of perjury for not being willing to venture a guess about what might have happened to the *Khian Sea*'s cargo of incinerator ash that had been offloaded somewhere by someone. From the very start, the prosecutors' schema was that Reilly (and also Dowd, in chapter 7) knew exactly what had happened to the ash and who was responsible for dumping it. It is only fair to assume that prosecutors hold a schema of guilt while the defense holds a schema of innocence, because that's what trials are all about. A serious problem arises, however, when the prosecution's schema rests on weak, unproven, or just plain faulty intelligence gathering. When the ship of schema begins to leak, it may be better to abandon ship than to foolishly try to sail ahead. The prosecutor was wise enough to do this in Senator Burris's case (chapter 12) and the district attorney came to the same conclusion in Father Sica's case (chapter 13).

3. Identify the agendas of the participants

There is no better way to determine what is foremost in a person's thinking than their conversational agendas (Shuy 1993, 39–40, 47–49, 165–66). In grand jury hearings, the venue for many perjury charges, the agendas of the participants are usually pretty clear. The prosecutor is trying to elicit evidence and the witness is either trying to give evidence or to avoid doing so. But the question/answer format in such speech events is not particularly useful for determining the participants' actual conversational agendas. However, when electronically recorded speech is used as evidence in perjury cases, the recordings are often good sources of the speakers' agendas. In three of the cases described earlier (chapters 5, 11, and 12), previously recorded conversations constituted the major evidence for the perjury charges.

The best evidence of a person's agenda is found in the topics they introduce and recycle as they talk. People bring up topics that are on their minds, and they tend not to introduce topics that are not. When they recycle their own topics later in the conversation, they reinforce their conversational agendas. In the same way, the topics that they do not bring up give evidence that such topics are not foremost on their agendas.

The efforts of the cooperating witness to get Kopp to admit that he originated the bank fraud (chapter 5) failed when Kopp simply didn't bring the topic up and when he responded to the cooperating witness's topics with answers that were off-topic. The same is true of lawyer Crow's handling of his client's recycled topics (chapter 11).

Space does not permit representing complete topic-analysis charts in chapters 5 and 11, but chapter 12 displays one for the brief telephone conversation between Senator Burris and the caller, showing that Burris's conversational agenda was not to purchase the Senate seat recently vacated by President Obama. It was not the senator's agenda in the only evidence the prosecution had.

4. Identify the responses to the questions asked to them

Responses to the topics or questions of the other participants can be equally instructive in providing clues to agendas (Shuy 1993, 39–40, 47–51, 102–4). Ignoring the other person's topic, changing the subject, not responding to it at all, or offering off-topic responses are all clues to intentions and agendas.

Kopp's responses to the cooperating witness's topics and questions (chapter 5) reveal much about what was and was not on his mind, as do Senator Burris's responses (chapter 12) as well as Father Sica's (chapter 13).

5. Determine how the participants use or fail to use the cooperative principle

H. P. Grice introduced the cooperative principle in 1967, with its maxims of quality (people are not expected to say anything they believe to be false or for which they lack adequate evidence), quantity (they are not expected to give less or more information than is needed), relation (they are not expected to say things that are irrelevant), and manner (they are expected to be brief and orderly, and not to be ambiguous or obscure). Implicatures arise from either following and flouting these maxims. In both grand jury hearings and ordinary conversations, participants expect these maxims to be followed. In the cases of Dowd (chapter 7) and Reilly (chapter 8), the prosecutors' questions flouted the maxims in ways that led the respondents to answer in a manner that led the jury to believe the men were guilty of perjury.

6. Identify the speech acts used by the participants

Requesting is one of several recognized speech acts (Searle 1969, 67). The speech act of asking questions is, of course, predominant in the cases that describe interrogations at trial or before a grand jury. If speakers want hearers to provide information, their questions must be first and foremost understandable and clear. What's more, the questioner and the answerer must have the same understanding of the words, expressions, phrases, and sentences in the questions. This requirement was far from met in the cases of the bankruptcy applicant (chapter 3), the state legislator (chapter 4), the undercover recordings of the businessman (chapter 5), the hunting license application (chapter 6), the grand jury testimony of the shipping executives (chapters 7 and 8), the questions put to the physician (chapter 9), the grand jury questions given the union representative (chapter 10), and the questions put to the priest (chapter 13).

Another type of requesting is the request for clarification, a frequently used speech act in human interaction. As noted earlier, obtaining clarification in courtroom exchanges is the primary responsibility of the lawyers who ask the questions, for they control and preserve the official record. The questions asked to the state legislator (chapter 4) could have been made clearer if the prosecutor had tried to resolve the ambiguities that emerged. These same problems existed in the cases of the two shipping executives (chapters 7 and 8). Unlike the prosecutors in their cases, they requested clarification several times in their grand jury hearings while for some reason the prosecutor chose not to do so. The union representative also tried to request clarification of the prosecutor's questions but was cut off by the prosecutor's hit-and-run strategy.

Before indictments are made and trials proceed, the intelligence analyst simply has to consider the existence and nature of the speech acts found in the evidence. Not doing this can lead to faulty indictments and convictions.

7. Notice the conversational strategies used by the participants

It's likely that the intelligence analyst will pay more attention to the language of the suspect than to the language of the government representative. This can be a big mistake, for the language of suspects is capable of being influenced by the ways the questions put to them are worded. In my book, *Creating Language Crimes,* I described a number of conversational strategies commonly used in undercover cases. These strategies are not unique to such cases; they occur in our everyday conversation, although not with the same legal implications.

The case of the union representative (chapter 10) illustrates the prosecutor's use of the hit-and-run strategy. Likewise, the recorded conversations in the case of the businessman (chapter 5) illustrate how the cooperating witness used the common strategies of hinting and retelling past events to try to get the businessman to agree with his propositions.

8. Pay close attention to the recency principle

When people try to disguise the import of what they are saying, they can couch their statement in complex sentences in which the crucial information is tucked away amidst one or more clauses that are perfectly benign. The effect on listeners is often to cause them to attend to the information in the main clause while ignoring the tucked-away or sometimes intentionally camouflaged crucial statement. In most of life, this makes little difference, but in legal contexts such as perjury cases, it can make the difference between innocence and guilt. We don't find problems with the recency principle very much in the trials, where lawyers are present to object to complex and unclear questions, but in perjury cases based on grand jury testimony, where no defense lawyer is present, the recency principle has lots of opportunities to occur. It can also occur in recorded conversations, where the opportunity to use the recency principle has a strong potential to occur. The cooperating witness taping his conversation with the businessman (chapter 5) provides a classic example of the disguised use of the recency principle.

9. Notice all ambiguous expressions and determine whether they were resolved

Violations of Grice's maxim of manner (be brief, orderly, and not ambiguous and obscure) are well illustrated in many of the cases in this book, including courtroom questions asked of the bankrupt businessman (chapter 3), the state politician (chapter 4), the shipping executives (chapters 7 and 8), and the physician (chapter 9). Recorded conversations used as evidence of perjury also provide examples, as in the cases of the lawyer/client interview (chapter 11) and the businessman's loan (chapter 5). In none of these cases did the government representative acknowledge the ambiguities or try to resolve them. Personal and relative pronouns are also often a rich source of ambiguity. By tracing the grammatical referencing, linguists can often untangle unclear uses of "it," "we," "that," and "you," especially when these words are seen in context.

10. Identify the words and expressions that are semantically significant in the case

We tend to believe that we understand and share the meanings of certain words and expressions that we use. But this is not always true, as revealed in the failure of both parties to have a meeting of the minds about the meaning of "income" (chapter 3), "reimburse" (chapter 4), "immediately prior to" and "residence" (chapter 6), "know," "what happened to," and "disposed of" (chapters 7 and 8), "recall," "organize," and "scab" (chapter 10), and "close personal relationship" (chapter 13). Failure to agree about how these words and expression were used and understood by each party led to serious problems in resolving these cases fairly. Again, it is the responsibility of the superordinate speaker in an exchange, the prosecutor, to first identify the fact that they are on different semantic wavelengths, and then to resolve the conflict of meaning. This mutual misunderstanding was neither identified nor resolved in any of the above cases.

To this point, I have not even mentioned the problems that arise when the suspect or defendant has only an imperfect knowledge of the language used at trial. The case of the Filipino-American physician (chapter 9) and the Hawaiian Creole–speaking union representative (chapter 10) provide many examples of the language and cultural interference that these men faced in their perjury cases.

My major point here, however, is that it would be prudent for the intelligence analysts, whether they are the prosecutor, the defense attorney, or the district attorney, to begin their intelligence analyses with the larger language units noted at the beginning of this list and to deal with the smaller language units as they are seen in the context of larger units. The individual words, phrases, or sentences may not be the smoking gun that they can seem to be on first appearance. And, if lawyers find this to be an insurmountable task, they can always call a linguist to help them.

REFERENCES

Andrews, Paul & Marilyn B. Peterson (eds.). 1990. *Criminal Intelligence Analysis*. Loomis CA: Palmer Enterprises.

Austin, J. L. 1962. *How To Do Things with Words*. Cambridge MA: Harvard U Press.

Berk-Seligson, Susan. 1990. *The Bilingual Courtroom*. Chicago: U of Chicago Press.

Berk-Seligson, Susan. 2009. *Coerced Confessions: The Discourse of Bilingual Police Interrogations*. Berlin: Mouton de Gruyter.

Bishop, Joel Prentiss. 1858. 2 *Commentaries on the Criminal Law*. Chicago: T.H. Flood.

Black's Law Dictionary. 6th ed. 2004. West Group.

Blakey, Robert. 1993. Forward (vi-xxii). In Roger W. Shuy, *Language Crimes*. Oxford: Blackwell.

Coleman, Linda & Paul Kay. 1981. Prototype semantics: The English word lie. *Language*, 57 (1): 26–44.

Coulthard, Malcolm & Alison Johnson (eds.). 2010. *Routledge Handbook of Forensic Linguistics*. London: Routledge.

Cuetos, F. & D. Mitchell. 1988. Cross-linguistic differences in parsing. *Cognition, 3:73–105*.

Eades, Diana. 1992. *Aboriginal English and the Law: Communication with Aboriginal English-Speaking Clients: A Handbook for Legal Practitioners*. Brisbane: Queensland Law Society.

Eades, Diana. 2008. *Courtroom Talk and Neocolonial Control*. Berlin: Mouton de Gruyter.

Ekman, Paul. 1985. *Telling Lies: Cures to Deceit in the Marketplace, Politics, and Marriage*. New York: Norton.

Fraser, Bruce. 1994. No conversation without misrepresentation (143–153). In Parret, H. (ed.) *Pretending to Communicate.* Berlin: Walter de Gruyter.

Freed, David. 2010. The wrong man. *The Atlantic* (May). 46–56.

Galasinski, Dariusz. 2000. *The Language of Deception: a Discourse Analytical Study.* Thousand Oaks CA: Sage.

Garner, Brian. 1995. *A Dictionary of Modern Legal Usage.* New York: Oxford U Press.

Gershman, Bennett. L. 1981. The perjury trap. *University of Pennsylvania Law Review.* Vol. 129:623–700.

Gibbons, John. 2003. *Forensic Linguistics: An Introduction to Language in the Justice System.* Oxford: Blackwell Publishing.

Gibson, Edward, Neal Pearlmutter, Eniqueta Cansco-Gonzales, & Gregory Hickok. 1996. *Recency Preference in the Human Sentence Processing Mechanism.* Amsterdam: Elsevier Science B.V.

Godfrey, Drexel E. & Don R. Harris. 1971. *Basic Elements of Intelligence.* Washington DC: U.S. Government Printing Office.

Grice, H. P. 1975. Logic and conversation. In Peter Cole & Jerry Morgan (eds.) *Syntax and Semantics,* Vol. 3 *Speech Acts.* New York: Cambridge U Press.

Gumperz, John. 1990. *Language and Social Identity.* New York: Cambridge U Press.

Hale, Sandra. 2004. *The Discourse of Court Interpreting: Discourse Practices of the Law, the Witness and the Interpreter.* Amsterdam: John Benjamins.

Harris, Don R. 1976. *Basic Elements of Intelligence.* Washington DC: U.S. Law Enforcement Assistance Administration.

Heuer, Richards J. Jr. 1999. Psychology of intelligence analysis. Washington DC: Center for the Study of Intelligence, Central Intelligence Agency.

Heymann, Phillip. 1984. FBI Undercover Operations (36–39), *Report of the Subcommittee on Civil and Constitutional Rights, 98th Congress, 2nd Session.* Washington DC: U.S. Government Printing Office.

Huddleston, Rodney & Geoffrey K. Pullum. 2002. *The Cambridge Grammar of the English Language.* Cambridge: Cambridge U Press.

Lucas, Ceil. 2003. *Language and the Law in Deaf Communities.* Washington DC: Gallaudet U Press.

Pauwels, A., M. D'Argaville, & D. Eades. 1992. Problems and issues of cross-cultural communication in legal settings (77–105). In Pauwels, A. (ed.) *Cross-cultural Comminication in Legal Settings.* Melbourne: Language and Society Centre, National Languages and Literacy Institute of Australia, Monash University,

Rummelhart, David E. 1975. Notes on a schema for stories. In Bobrow, D. G. & A. M. Collins (eds.) *Representation and Understanding: Studies in Cognitive Science.* New York: Academic Press.

Searle, John R. 1969. *Speech Acts: An Essay in the Philosophy of Language.* Cambridge: Cambridge U Press.

Shuy, Roger W. 1982. Topic as the unit of analysis in a criminal law case. In Tannen, Deborah (ed.) *Analyzing Discourse: Text and Talk.* Washington DC: Georgetown U Press.

Shuy, Roger W. 1990. The analysis of tape recorded conversations. In Andrews, Paul & Marilyn B. Peterson (eds.) *Criminal Intelligence Analysis.* Loomis CA: Palmer Enterprises, 117–48.

Shuy, Roger W. 1993. *Language Crimes.* Oxford: Blackwell.

Shuy, Roger W. 1998a. *The Language of Confession, Interrogation, and Deception.* Thousand Oaks CA: Sage Publications.

Shuy, Roger W. 1998b. *Bureaucratic Language in Government and Business.* Washington DC: Georgetown U Press.

Shuy, Roger W. 2001. Discourse analysis in the legal context. In Schiffrin, Deborah, Deborah Tannen & Heidi Hamilton (eds.) *The Handbook of Discourse Analysis.* Oxford: Blackwell, 437–52.

Shuy, Roger W. 2005. *Creating Language Crimes: How Law Enforcement Uses (and Misuses) Language.* New York: Oxford U Press.

Shuy, Roger W. 2010. Linguistics and Terrorism Cases. In Coulthard, Malcolm & Alison Johnson (eds.) *Routledge Handbook of Forensic Linguistics.* London: Routledge, 558–75.

Solan, Lawrence & Peter Tiersma. 2005. *Speaking of Crime.* Chicago: U of Chicago Press.

Tiersma, Peter. 1990. The language of perjury: "Literal truth," ambiguity, and the false statement requirement. *Southern California Law Review*: 62–63, 373–431.

Tiersma, Peter. 1999. *Legal Language.* Chicago: U Chicago Press.

Van Dijk, Teun A. 1985. *Handbook of Discourse Analysis.* New York: Academic Press.

CASES CITED

United States District Court, District of New Jersey v. Larry Kopp Criminal No. 89-264 (CSF).

Commonwealth of Pennsylvania in the Court of Common Pleas, Dauphin County, Pennsylvania v. Joseph F. Sica No. 22-MD-2008.

United States District Court for the Eastern District of Pennsylvania v. William P. Reilly Criminal No. 93-039.

United States District Court for the District of Delaware v. John Patrick Dowd Criminal No. 92-53.

United States District Court for the Northern District of Texas v. William White Bolles Criminal No. 3-95CR-031-H.

United States District Court for the Middle District of Pennsylvania v. Frank Serafini Criminal No. 3: CR-97-225.

State of Montana Fourteenth Judicial District Court, Musselshell County v. Randoph A. Turpin Cause No. DC-06-23.

United States District Court of Honolulu v. Stephen Suyat.

United States District Court of Kansas City v. Donald Crow.

United States v. Dunnigan, 507 U.S. 87, 94 (1993).

United States District Court Central District of California, Los Angeles v. John Z. DeLorean No. 83-7670.

United States v. Mandujano, 425 U.S. 564, 581-82 (1976).

Bronston v. United States, 409 U.S. 352, 353 (1973).

Duckworth v. District Court, 107 M 97, 80 P2d 367 (1938).

Brogan v. United States, 552 U.S. 398, (1998).

Blair v. United States, 250 U.S. 282 (1919).

INDEX

Printed and bound by CPI Group (UK) Ltd, Croydon, CR0 4YY